This book reclaims pedagogy as a theoretical field of study by exploring the mutually enhancing interaction of critical theory and pedagogy. The essayists use theory to read the classroom in its institutional context, to read the actual content and assignments of composition courses—in short, to interpret the rhetoric of teaching.

The essayists investigate the pedagogical agenda implied in the theories of particular writers—Barthes, Lacan, Burke, for example—and transform and resituate them in the classroom. The book does not advocate a single method of instruction, but instead reminds us that theory is continually modified by institutions and classroom practices.

Patricia Donahue is Assistant Professor of English at Lafayette College, Easton, Pennsylvania.

Ellen Quandahl is Assistant Professor of English at the University of Southern California.

D1206007

Reclaiming Pedagogy: The Rhetoric of the Classroom

Patricia Donahue
& Ellen Quandahl

Southern Illinois University Press
Carbondale and Edwardsville

Library of Congress Cataloging-in-Publication Data

Reclaiming pedagogy: the rhetoric of the classroom / edited by
   Patricia Donahue and Ellen Quandahl.
      p.   cm.
   Bibliography: p.
   Includes index.
   ISBN 0-8093-1534-3
   1. English language—Rhetoric—Study and teaching. 2. Literature—
History and criticism—Theory, etc.   I. Quandahl, Ellen M.
II. Donahue, Patricia, 1953–
PE1404.R38   1989

808'.042'07—dc19   88-39324
                                                                CIP

Designed by Shannon M. McIntyre
Production supervised by Natalia Nadraga

92   91   90   89   4   3   2   1

The paper used in this publication meets the minimum requirements of
American National Standard for Information Sciences —Permanence of
Paper for Printed Library Materials, ANSI Z39.48-1984. ∞

Contents

Acknowledgments

We would like to thank all our colleagues at Lafayette College and the University of Southern California who have been helpful with this project. We also thank our colleagues in the Freshman Preparatory Program at UCLA, where this book began, Richard Lanham, who envisioned innovative pedagogy in UCLA Writing Programs, and Lauren Cammack, whose intelligent administration made it possible to do the work. Mike Rose had faith in our project from the start, and his confidence in our work means a great deal to us. For their careful readings of portions of the manuscript, we are especially grateful to Lawrence Green, Donna Gregory, Gracia Grindal, James Kincaid, Richard Regosin, Lee Upton, and Ross Winterowd. We thank all of the contributors to this collection, who were also generous readers. We thank our editor, Kenney Withers, for his guidance and encouragement, and Jill Reifenstahl for her assistance in preparing the manuscript. And we owe special thanks to Larry Wheeler and Mike Garst for their friendship and support.

Contributors

Lori Chamberlain, Ph.D., is a student at Boalt Hall School of Law, University of California, Berkeley.

Michael Clark, Ph.D., is Associate Professor of English and Comparative Literature at the University of California, Irvine.

Patricia Donahue, Ph.D., is Assistant Professor of English at Lafayette College, Easton, Pennsylvania.

Dennis A. Foster, Ph.D., is Associate Professor of English at Southern Methodist University.

Jon Klancher, Ph.D., is Assistant Professor of English at Boston University.

Randall Knoper, Ph.D., is Assistant Professor of English at Lafayette College, Easton, Pennsylvania.

Elaine O. Lees, Ph.D., is a consultant to the Pittsburgh Board of Public Education and a member of the Carlow Hill College Faculty.

Ellen Quandahl, Ph.D., is Assistant Professor of English at the University of Southern California.

Mariolina Salvatori, Ph.D., is Associate Professor of English at the University of Pittsburgh.

Nina Schwartz, Ph.D., is Assistant Professor of English at Southern Methodist University.

Reclaiming Pedagogy

1

Reading the Classroom

*Patricia Donahue and
Ellen Quandahl*

In this opening chapter, we offer a prologue to the book—an introduction to its content and description of its themes—and we examine uses of the literature called critical theory in composition studies.[1] Critical theory, as many before us have remarked, is no stranger to teachers of writing, and has been called upon to satisfy a range of aims. We want to read the map of those aims, so as to make claims about our profession's desires and commitments. But the real subject here is a new wave of composition research, encouraging us to read classroom practice through critical theory, and promising, moreover, a mutually enhancing interaction of theory and pedagogy.

This book, in the broadest possible sense, represents an effort to "reclaim" pedagogy as a theoretical field of study, a critical practice. The essays either examine pedagogy as a theoretical field or investigate the pedagogical subtensions of a specific theory. Rather than advocate a single method of instruction, they remind us of the range of possibilities that have emerged from developments in theory "after the new criticism," and that remain extremely valuable.

We are well aware that this book is not the first to situate pedagogy in the context of critical theory or to explore the possible connections between theory and composition. Some very fine work along these lines has recently been published in journals and influential collec-

1

tions like *Composition and Literature: Bridging the Gap; Theory in the Classroom; Writing and Reading Differently;* and *Only Connect: Uniting Reading and Writing,* and it has received well-deserved attention. Our book builds on that work and is indebted to it, and it also makes a conscious attempt to read practice through theory and to invite speculation about the practical uses of theory in the classroom. In our early discussions about this book, we felt that the acid test, what would really distinguish it from others recently published, would be its ability to offer very concrete realizations of theory that nonetheless retain the sophistication and bite of the theoretical discussion. We know how justly impatient our compositionist colleagues—who daily face inexperienced student writers and intransigent administrations—have been with gestures toward poststructuralist and other pedagogies that with fancy language merely repackage what we have always done. On the other hand we are keenly aware that a concrete pedagogy of a deconstructive, semiotic, or otherwise revisionary variety might be read as mere technique, or as an attempt at innovation for its own sake, if in any way cut off from less local debates about the ideologies that justify teaching and scholarship and their allocation into disciplines, about the role of writing in the university, and about ways in which writing courses support institutions that should not themselves stand free from criticism.

With these issues in mind, we have collected essays that use critical theory to read the classroom in its institutional context, to read the language of teaching, to read student essays, and to read the actual content and assignments of composition courses—in short, essays that examine the rhetoric of teaching. And we make two claims for this book as a voice in discussions of theory, pedagogy, and composition research: first, that theory can produce crucial changes in the assumptions and practices of composition teachers; second, that theory is no monolith but a productive agency that is itself modified when engaged in reading the classroom. Although we consistently use *theory* in the singular in this chapter, the contributors offer a plurality of theoretical/pedagogical approaches. Theory, after all, is not unified, nor should be its uses. There is no single pedagogy that emerges from these pages, but rather a number of possibilities that fundamentally have in common the desire to turn the insights of theory onto the scene of instruction itself.

The point for us is that composition pedagogy "interacts" (an important word) with theory; it does not submit to theory. As analytical readers of theoretical texts, compositionists transform what they find. And because they value pedagogy, their transformations are "teacherly." That is, they uncover and modify theory's submerged pedagogical agenda, resituating it in classrooms where reading and writing—discourse—are intensively taught.

The essays in this volume share a "teacherly" perspective and a series of common principles. First, these pedagogies are very textual, text-oriented. At the heart of the composition course, the contributors repeatedly claim, is the written product and the reader's (the student's as well as the teacher's) act of interpreting and criticizing it. This emphasis on interpreting and criticizing—on *analyzing*—is in no way an apology for teaching theory or literature, what many suppose to be the real love of composition teachers, what they secretly hanker to do. Rather, it is an attempt to grapple with the fact that, as Nina Schwartz puts it, "attention to reading often conflicts with or even impedes the teaching of more explicitly 'practical' writing skills." Clearly there is an emphasis on texts in these essays, even a localized reading of texts, that may strike our readers as hardly new. But the goal of reading closely is not to establish coherence but to turn attention to language as a system of power and to the reader as a constituent of that system. Lori Chamberlain, for example, shows the political relation between the writer and an audience addressed or excluded in a particular trope, irony.

The kind of reading described here can best be characterized as "resistant reading." Students are encouraged to resist the argument of a text, the influence of common sense, or even the teacher's authority over learning—that is, to resist the monologic voice that depends for its meaning upon readers' thoroughly sharing the assumptions of writers. Unambiguous readings exclude interpretations made by marginalized or oppositional readers; but to reveal multiple readings—as resistant reading does—allows variously circulating interpretive codes to come into play. People outside the dominant interpretive system are not silenced. There is an effort, then, to make interpretation less mysterious by making the processes of reading explicit, and helping students to be more aware, more reflexive, about their own readings. The aim is not to awaken the ideologically complacent, but to teach ways in which discursive authority functions.

It must be added that such teaching does not "free" students, but demonstrates how components of ideological systems come to appear as "choices" and "freedoms." And furthermore, as Bourdieu would show, that resistant reading is a "good" or even "meaningful" practice is also generated by a particular framework of dispositions. The contributors, therefore, are also aware that their own positions are culturally determined. As Patricia Donahue argues, "in teaching cultural critique, we must not become blind to the ideology of our own position."

Second, critical analysis is defined as an act of power and language as the site of a struggle to determine "truth" and to control its production. Having accepted this premise, these essays examine the distribution of power in classrooms as well as in texts, and they examine the power of institutions both to restrain and to enable nontraditional instructional approaches. There is no escape from but only opportunities to understand—or begin to understand—the conditions of power. One move in that regard is a transfer of power from teacher to student through the recognition of the student as *competent,* rich in resources, culturally knowledgeable (even if this knowledge is not fully articulated). As Mariolina Salvatori comments, "Inquiry becomes a rigorously structured collaborative activity . . . that calls for a visible, structural change in the realignment of the teacher/student interaction. . . . This interaction is made possible by and makes possible the recognition of a student's work as a form of knowledge in the process of formation. This interaction makes it possible for student and teacher to get to know each other, and to recognize each other as more than instantiations of roles." The point is made again and again that teachers must begin where the students are, that teachers themselves are students in the classroom, constantly being taught by those—the students—who know how they can learn.

Third, these essays acknowledge the pressures exerted upon writing by both culture and the body, and they consider the influence of desire as well as reason upon the writing activity. They examine the irrational and mysterious, explore uncharted—and sometimes disturbing—ground. Dennis A. Foster, for example, looks at ways in which teachers and texts resemble Lacan's powerful Subject Supposed to Know, and asks, "how can one move beyond the initially motivating, but ultimately obscuring power of transference?"

Finally, these essays recognize—through the complexity of their discussions and their frames of reference—the generally acknowledged sophistication of the composition audience. They make no attempt to introduce the reader to Lacan or to soften the experience of understanding difficult material—such work is readily available. Instead, they assume some knowledge of theory, frequently providing only fragments of theoretical texts, and they build on that knowledge. These essays, like many others being written today, offer creative fusions of critical theory and composition pedagogy. In their effort to read practice through the theories they favor, they create an interaction between theory and composition that can have a transformative effect on instruction—or so we hope our readers will conclude.

In the following sections we will characterize in greater detail the features of interactive pedagogies and the distance that separates them from other uses of theory in the classroom. And since these pedagogies are very much centered in composition and are a part of its controversial development, we examine their relationship to other intellectual movements within the field, specifically, social constructionism and the emphasis upon academic conventions.

Application/Affiliation/Interaction

Earlier we claimed that theory and composition interact, or rather *should* interact. But often they do not. Critical theory may be used to justify newly orthodox practices or to improve composition's status as an academic discipline. We use the term *interact* to distinguish what we regard as self-reflexive, self-critical pedagogies from those that promote theory at the expense of composition and composition at the expense of theory. We refer to those efforts as "application" and "affiliation," and we will begin by defining them.

Most often, theory is applied to composition in order to correct the flaws of each. While critical theory is valued for its abstractions, it is also criticized for its inaccessibility and resistance to practice. And while composition is praised for its attention to method, it is said to lack a coherent conceptual system and a stable disciplinary center. The solution seems simple: apply theory to composition. The composition classroom can then be used to provide theory with substantial and concrete proof of its arguments, and theory can be used to provide composition with a metadiscourse, the means to explain itself. This solution is finally unsatisfying. When theory is discussed and then illustrated with a classroom exercise or when a classroom practice is theoretically justified, theory and composition remain unaffected by each other. They run in parallel lines.

The same lack of interaction is present in affiliation. Affiliative work attempts to make composition less peripheral by aligning it, or claiming a *filial* relationship, with the body of work that carries the most weight in English departments these days. The argument is that composition resembles and even mirrors theory because it shares its beliefs in the epistemology of process, the function of textuality, and the significance of writing. In fact, some affiliative studies go so far as to say that composition was ahead of its time. While colleagues in literature were skeptical of the radical material imported from abroad, compositionists embraced it. In a sense, they already knew it. The lessons about writing that theory had to teach held no surprises for teachers of writing. The motive for affiliation, finally, is simple: to use theory to justify what we already do. But our point is not that composition requires justification through a thematic linking of process pedagogy with theory. As the new work in composition demonstrates, critical theory offers us a voice that lets us hear ourselves: a way to interpret and revise our own practices.

However, to those who stand in the middle of great paradigm shifts, composition studies may appear diffuse and heterogeneous, a confusing assemblage of competing practices. And this poses a problem. For if, as tradition dictates, a shared problematic and a set of questions defines a discipline, do we have a discipline? In affiliative studies, the means for disciplinary coherence, definition, and commonality are to be found in critical theory, because it offers a rich and plunderable language, a privileged center. But when theory is used for such justification, something is lost—diversity and potential for change. In a time when theorists are questioning the notion of integrated, disciplinary "knowledge" that is in agreement with itself, and attempting to introduce difference into pedagogy (Ulmer 160), it is ironic that there should be this move to give composition the status, the prestige, of a monolithic discipline. Perhaps it is for the best that we lack a subject matter, a content that can be mastered and exhausted. As Gorgias told Socrates, our subject is simply *words* (*Gorgias* 449c). If that is the case, then diversity may be our strong point, as that which has the power to disturb normative methods. Affiliative work, then, would be self-defeating—a tendency to use only what is "good" in theory (the easy and familiar) and to ignore the "bad" (the unfamiliar, heterogeneous, disruptive). But if critical theory is as powerful as everyone says, should we not use it to resee what we do, rather than to affirm what we have done?

To resee what we do is precisely the aim of the interactive pedagogies in this volume. Generally speaking, the frameworks they employ for this activity are to be found in Continental philosophers of historicist and anti-idealist bent (Heidegger, Nietzsche, Marx, Freud), transformed and rearticulated by Derrida, Barthes, Lacan, Bakhtin, Burke, and Foucault. Several of the essays also draw on philosophies problematically known as "reader-response" theory, which they critique even as they call upon it. To generalize a bit further (and this will be obvious to many of our readers), many of these rearticulations also draw upon a language of linguistics—that of Peirce and Saussure, for example. Thus, they focus on the historicity of knowledge, and also on its emergence from a play of differences, from a play of signs endlessly referring to other signs, even as they show how this free play is arrested by conventions and the demands of a discipline. The view of human subjectivity suggested by all of the essays is that we are motivated by desire as well as reason, and that while we are active in the production of meaning, we may never control the meanings we produce. Consequently, we must examine a text's silences as well as its blatant assertions and consider—as thoroughly as we can—the extent to which we are spoken by forces within us.

The relationship of interactive pedagogies to their philosophical predecessors and newly canonized authorities is, in Foucault's understanding of the distinction, genealogical rather than historical. That is, they do not turn to their predecessors to demonstrate, as Foucault would say, "an unbroken continuity" ("Nietzsche" 146). They do not look for origins or justifications, for applications or affiliations. They attempt instead to "excavate" theory and philosophy, to examine their many strata, to reconstruct the pieces they find. They plunder—but with a motive: to rewrite theoretical texts, to make the pedagogies explicit, and to read classroom practice through theory.

We want to make clear that these "interactive pedagogies" are solidly anchored in composition and participate in its ongoing debates. Nonetheless, they are frequently silent on the subject of process pedagogy and shifting paradigms. As the newly orthodox, *process* is a cliché now. It is time to respond to the repressions engendered by the process model, repressions that come from claiming revolutionary status for this model and from forgetting the significant similarities between it and the traditional model of product. Our profession may have confused "revolution" (Kuhn's theory of radical scientific change) with "redistributed transformation" (Foucault's account of the reassignment of value to elements in a binary pair). As a result, many process models, like the product models before them, continue to recommend the teaching of serviceable prose and to define the writer as autonomous, freely willed, and in control of his or her choices. More broadly speaking, it is necessary to address how our disciplinary paradigms have worked to inhibit as well as to enable change. In the following section, we will look at one of those disciplinary paradigms—social construction—and consider how interactive pedagogies revise its concept of the social reproduction of knowledge.

Social Construction and the Problem of Reproduction

One disciplinary axis on which interactive pedagogies both place and "displace" their work is the pedagogical perspective Lester Faigley has called the "social view," sometimes also called "social constructionism." In this view, the "individual is a constituent of culture" (Faigley 535), and "The terms in which the world is understood are social artifacts, products of historically situated interchanges among people" (Gergen 267). The essayists in this volume and the writers they cite are social constructionists of the deepest hue, claiming that we are always already within a historical context that shapes beliefs and practices. They do not, however, draw on certain writers whose work has already thoroughly infiltrated composition: Thomas Kuhn in science, Berger and Luckmann in sociology, Clifford Geertz in anthropology, Richard Rorty in philosophy, and Kenneth Bruffee in English. This distinction is evident in the fact that these essays do not have as their aim the reproduction of the social constructionist conclusion—that the classroom is to be *modeled* on a particular representation of how ideas are justified and "knowledge" generated. In Bruffee, for example, the writing class is to be a conversation, since writing itself is a kind of conversation, technologically displaced. These essays neither advocate the teaching of theory per se, nor ask students to reproduce the claims of the theorists who inform their pedagogy. Unlike Rorty, whose new pragmatism relies on hammering home the conclusion that knowledge is socially justified and adjudicated, these writers take for granted that this nail is already in place, and move on.

Indeed, these essayists question not only the desirability but the possibility of intentionally producing the social processes that generate knowledge. They view such processes as much more complex than the conversation metaphor—a picture of thinkers exchanging and adjusting ideas in community—allows. Refusing conversation or speech as originary, they suggest that any learning—whether organized conversationally, collaboratively, or in the most authoritarian manner—is social, and its socialness is beyond conscious reproduction. It is imbricated, to use Foucault's words, in "the double articulation of this history of individuals upon the unconscious of culture, and the historicity of those cultures upon the unconscious of individuals" (*Order* 379). Interactive pedagogies are less interested in the fact of socialness (a fact they take as given) than in particular kinds of socialness, the cultural inscriptions in any text, including the pedagogical scene.

Another way in which interactive pedagogies move beyond social constructionism, while sharing its commitment to socialness, is by directing attention less to models of thinking than to representations of thought in texts—texts by students as well as professional writers. They are concerned with what Kenneth Burke calls empirical evidence, the demonstrable, readily observable relationships in texts (57–58). This attention to textuality raises questions about discursive authority, which in turn call for examining particular uses of social, ideological theory in the classroom. Once more the theme of reproduction comes into play. Most writing teachers are all too familiar with students who, as Jon Klancher argues, are "immune to the surprises" of ideological critique. A popular assignment in high school English classes is an analysis of TV advertising, and students have learned their lesson well: they will reproduce, as often as we like, the conclusion about advertising's invidious influence on consumer desires. This reproduction of preexisting "truth" is not just our students' problem. When writing teachers talk about critical thinking, they may simply be talking about urging students from the conservative ideology now in ascendancy to a more liberal one they themselves hold. As Ellen Quandahl suggests, claims that "students' readings are rigid, conservative and commonplace . . . ignore the extent to which pedagogy has ignored the performative aspect of texts." Interactive pedagogies, therefore, involve reading the text of our own pedagogical discourse to examine how, even there, education naturalizes the social, and to remind us that, while our language can never be neutral, our aim is to teach the composing and recomposing of texts that constitutes interpretation, not liberal thinking.

Conventions/Contexts/Content

Our use of the words *reading strategies* in the last section suggests that interpretation, like composing, involves conventions, is a conventional activity. The topic of conventions is one that has dominated composition work much more than, say, discussion about the content or subject matter of readings for composition classes. In the writing across the curriculum movement, for example, Elaine Maimon has urged that we need to identify and teach the specific discourse conventions of the various disciplines. David Bartholomae has argued that composition teachers could identify the general conventions of academic prose, since it is their lack of familiarity with these that prevents students from entering academic discourse. The essayists in this book, however, do not claim to identify either the specific conventions of a discipline or the general conventions of the university that could then serve as heuristics (and which, under the guise of convention, would be easily hypostatized as rules). Rather, their collective suggestion is that the texts and problems of a composition course should provide or build up some interpretive frameworks through which the students will read and write.

Although these interpretive frameworks are not situated within a single discipline, we argue that they are content-bound. (If that content is of unmistakable consequence, so much the better; we are not arbiters of consequence, nor do we enter the debate about canon.) In this we differ from the recent rhetorical tradition, with its deployment of *topoi* and heuristics, and recent work in the cognitive sciences, with their information-processing strain, both of which have tended to separate strategies, planning, and articulation of goals from content. One hope of those who separate technique from content is that composition could provide an introduction into the liberal arts curriculum and that there would be "carry-over": the heuristic methods taught in composition would transfer into the writing students do in other university and even nonuniversity settings. Consider, for example, Flower and Hayes' well-known diagram of writing processes, a rich metaphor of serial processing, with built-in recursions. It is content blind. Planning, in this model, is building an internal representation of knowledge, which is stored in the writer's long-term memory, as it is to be used in the paper. To put their case starkly, writing, then, is primarily acts of recoding stored knowledge. In our view, this and other "content-neutral" heuristics ignore the added complexities of reading the difficult texts that are necessarily part of the investigative and interpretive writing demanded in the university, and that are of special value in a culture dominated by uncritical absorption of media messages.

Let us separate out several issues around our interest in content, beginning with its relation to interpretation. First, as Foucault says, ". . . interpretation is the violent or surreptitious appropriation of a system of rules, which itself has no essential meaning, in order to impose a direction, to bend it to a new will, to force its participation in a different game, and to subject it to secondary rules" ("Nietzsche"

151–52). In asking students to interpret texts in their compositions, then, we are asking them to assert power, to own rules, and to shape a new content. This content, while new to them, is not the product of genius or discovery, but a reweaving of textual threads into new patterns.

A second issue is that several of these essays stress the need to teach students to read content contextually. The context of reading is primarily cultural, and these teachers are archivists: they bring culture into the classroom. Following Derrida and others they re-form class space as social space, and identify the crossings between the two. At the same time, whatever interpretive conventions a text offers are also themselves context- and content-bound. Students reading Freud, as Donahue and Quandahl show, learn not only certain psychoanalytic "moves" that are a product of Freud's psychoanalytic approach, but that this approach, these psychoanalytic conventions, also arise out of Freud's experience "as a nineteenth-century male, husband, and father." Students need a historical perspective, a sense of their difference, so they can understand the history of the present. This is not to say that composition involves detailed exegeses of historical matter; after all, it is not a "humanities" course. Yet it can effectively introduce the process of excavation, of seeing texts as having many interrelated strata. In fact, it will be successful if it does little more than give students the experience of encountering difficult texts and interpreting them in writing through the frameworks of knowledge and points of view those very texts allow them to develop.

Finally, the content, the meaning, of texts is also shaped by the knowledge students bring to those texts. This is, of course, one of the major themes of reader-response theory, and an idea that permeates *Reclaiming Pedagogy*. It is not surprising that the curricula described in this book pay a great deal of attention to the ideas and methods students bring to the classroom. And in so doing, they share something of the ethos, or perhaps we should say the style, that distinguishes the best composition teaching today.

Student-centered pedagogies flourish, branching from the work of Mina Shaughnessy, Paulo Freire, the varieties of ideological interpretation that would question authority, and the general wisdom of a decade ago, that the course should meet students where they are, empower them, make them comfortable and confident. The idea that students would write better—more compellingly, with greater engagement and liveliness, and with fewer errors—if they write about subjects close to themselves, is not new. It was urged by Theodore

Baird in the 1930s, and has been urged by his student Walker Gibson and Gibson's student William Coles. Wayne Booth, in an article that has become one of the touchstones of the field, "The Rhetorical Stance," made a similar point in more traditionally rhetorical terms. Personal writing is strongly urged by W. Ross Winterowd in *Contemporary Rhetoric,* another milestone text that helped to consolidate composition as a field of inquiry. Nowhere is it more evident than in CCC's 1974 statement, "Students' Right to Their Own Language." It is present in James Britton's notion of an "expressive matrix," language close to the self from which all discourse, even the most public writing, grows, and in Linda Flower's *writer-based* prose, the egocentric writing that students must translate into audience-aware, reader-based prose.

In a general sense, the essays in this volume concur with the wisdom of this still-growing body of literature: students, their ideas, their experiences, and their dialects are to be respected. Elaine O. Lees suggests, quoting Fish, that "one teaches someone the interpretive strategies of a community new to him, that is, by 'backing up' to interpretive procedures the teacher and learner share." We see students as culturally competent, as survivors who in their lifetimes have accumulated many kinds of strategies for successfully negotiating cultural systems. While their repertoires may not be as large as expert writers' and while they may not always know how to use these strategies, they do possess them.

What distinguishes the "personal" element in these pedagogies is the understanding that students have a great deal of knowledge, knowledge that is ideologically charged, simply because they have entered the symbolic (which is not personal at all). This phrase, "entered the symbolic," recalls theories of language articulated by people like Lacan, Kristeva, and Althusser. Put simply, the symbolic order of culture is its collective set of signifying systems, one of which is language, and language is a system that preexists the individual. The individual enters that system at a particular stage of development, uses it to produce meaning, and is produced by it. That is, as Kaja Silverman has said, "the discourse within which the subject finds its identity is always the discourse of the Other—of a symbolic order which transcends the subject, and which orchestrates its entire history" (194). In other words, as any person, any "subject," begins to learn language, that person is shaped by and "knows" negation, desire, exclusion, patterns of cultural prohibitions and sanctions and the institutions that support and legitimate them. The teacherly perspective looks to this deoriginating knowledge.

We might consider, for purposes of comparison and to bring this point more sharply into focus, one of the best known student-centered pedagogies. Peter Elbow has argued that "everyone can, under certain conditions, speak with clarity and power." Coaching this native eloquence is a matter of encouraging two skills, "the ability to create words and ideas out of yourself," and the ability to "criticize them in order to decide which ones to use." In contrast to this view, we would argue that there is no such thing as creating words out of yourself, since subjectivity, one's self, is a social order, preexisting the individual. And criticizing is not so much a matter of "taking what's good and discarding what isn't" (Elbow 7) as shaping and extending the tropes of other discourses. One enters rather than generates a textual history. Thus, the new student-centered pedagogies do not claim that students must learn to write in their own voice, as if there were a self-originating language, or that students must write about their familiar social life, if they are to write with confidence. Knowledge, as we have said, is cultural and relational, consisting of patterns and figures that students to a large extent already posses. But as Schwartz points out, "Students . . . can hardly be expected to exemplify in their own writing a sophisticated understanding of why they think one thing rather than another until they have learned to see their views as something other than inevitable." The teacher's role is to prompt the recognition and naming of used and unidentified discourse strategies, strategies often seen as natural rather than social. The teacher possesses what Foucault calls a "counter-memory," foregrounding techniques as acquired strategies.

The Politics of Teaching

In this last section, we would like to begin by saying the obvious: for the teacher to act as "counter-memory" is not that easy. Beyond the fact that teachers deeply involved with composition who are also willing to engage the language of critical theory are understandably few (and that, finally, is why "bridging the gap" is so difficult), there is this more complex issue: there is "always already" theory in the classroom. Just as graduate students who complete their introductory course in critical theory will readily revert to thematic reading, to using the theory they know like breathing, teachers aware of poststructuralism will revert to "working on students' writing," to teaching clean, clear, coherent prose, to aligning theory with the orthodoxies already in place. We should say unequivocally that we and the contributors to this collection are not talking about "working on students' writing." Not because, as those who settled the grammar issue have taught us (and they are right), it does no good, but because learning to write conventionally ("correctly") is at odds with reading complicatedly. By writing conventionally we mean using the rhetorical modes the textbooks continue to promote (moving, for example, from narration to exposition), reading for and writing thesis sentences, emphasizing unity and managing ambiguity. Such injunctions lead to prose that suppresses conflict and encourages the unconscious reproduction of social norms (self-control, for example). While we do not argue for unintelligibility (yet recognizing that standards of intelligibility change and are historically conditioned) we do urge a revision of standards, a bringing up-to-date so that practices can match the new epistemologies of our age.

Let us be specific about this revision. The argument we are making is related to one already made by Gregory Ulmer in his discussion of Derrida's post-Hegelian pedagogy. Glossing Derrida, Ulmer says,

> The problem that Hegel wishes to efface is that of the relation of the order of inquiry to the order of exposition (*Darstellung*). Hegel, typifying the bias of logocentrism, imagines or idealizes a writing in which "there would be no discrepancy between production and exposition, only a *presentation* of the concept by itself, in its own words, in its own logos. . . ." (161)

For Derrida, of course, exposition always exceeds or adds to what it presents. This is the curious logic of the *supplement,* and it is an important revision, for philosophy, of the idea that a body of philosophical tradition and knowledge is simply transmitted in the classroom. But what does it mean for composition, where exposition rather than transmission has always been the primary concern? We believe that the new methods of reading neither dictate the composing of postmodern pastiches (which could simply be accomplished through old-fashioned *imitatio,* anyway), nor promote disregard for attention to prose at the "sentence-level." And yet, there is in these essays a definite shift in attention, analogous to "de-centered" reading. For one thing, the writers, quite apart from new theory, have taken composition researchers at their word; they have taken the dare not to edit, indeed to revise our understanding of editing, and they show what to do in that crucial space in the course when one is not marking a single error. They teach students to revise content, ideas, by giving assignments that teach them how to look at the material they are interpreting in a new way, that draw attention to the excesses, the supplementarity of that material. These essays, then, focus neither on simple reproduction or exposition, but on the inexhaustibility of the text. If, as Randall Knoper argues, "embedded in our best writing is an education about writing itself—its figurative, rhetorical, shifting capacities, its provisional place in the interweavings of other writings—then we are right to share this education with our students." The problem we are trying to get at is this: in spite of the strong rhetoric of subversion in many of the theorists cited in this volume, we know that there is even stronger institutional pressure to align new theory with the known.

We have named that pressure more broadly as the demands of inflexible disciplines upon an interdisciplinary body of theory. More broadly still, institutions exert pressure upon classroom practice. Critical theory offers an agenda of radical change that could challenge the foundation of American education. It is thus not surprising that theory is often distorted or neutralized when injected into the pedagogical scene. We are living in a time of stasis when conservatism is revered and diversity, transformation, and analysis are seen as further evidence of the "closing of the American mind." Society is increasing its demand that students prepare for citizenship by producing normative and serviceable prose, language suitable for the information age. The writers in this volume resist the move to teach cultural literacy, to reproduce traditional wisdom. They refuse to dilute theory and to neutralize its power to demystify. They want to give students specific analytical methods for reading the world, for understanding the terms of linguistic power, for resisting oppressive authority. To be sure, students who leave these "theorized" classrooms may eventually be reappropriated and once again accept the myths of common sense. But for a semester or two, they will have had the opportunity to see differently. The chance to make a difference, to read practice through theory, and to reclaim pedagogy as a theoretical field is the chance we in composition seek. Efforts to use theory to promote an agenda of change, a change that comes through reflecting as well as doing, are in many ways visionary. While it may be bold to declare the new work in composition as visionary, this is an age that requires boldness. And so we invite our readers to consider the following essays and all the new and provocative work being done in composition in an equally audacious light.

Notes

1. Like Andreas Huyssen, we "follow the current usage in which the term 'critical theory' refers to a multitude of recent theoretical and interdisciplinary endeavors in the humanities. Originally, critical theory was a much more focused term that referred to the theory developed by the Frankfurt School since the 1930's. Today, however, the critical theory of the Frankfurt School is itself only part of an expanded field of critical theories" (36).

Works Cited

Burke, Kenneth. *A Grammar of Motives*. Berkeley: U of California P, 1969.

Elbow, Peter. *Writing With Power*. New York: Oxford UP, 1981.

Faigley, Lester. "Competing Theories of Process: A Critique and a Proposal." *College English* 48.6 (1986): 527–24.

Foucault, Michel. "Nietzsche, Genealogy, History." *Language, Counter-Memory, Practice*. Ed. Donald F. Bouchard. Ithaca, NY: Cornell UP, 1977. 139–64.

———. *The Order of Things*. New York: Random, 1970.

Gergen, Kenneth J. "The Social Constructionist Movement in Modern Psychology." *American Psychologist* 40.3 (1985): 266–75.

Huyssen, Andreas. "Mapping the Postmodern." *New German Critique* 33 (1984): 5–52.

Silverman, Kaja. *The Subject of Semiotics*. New York: Oxford UP, 1983.

Ulmer, Gergory L. *Applied Grammatology: Post(e)-Pedagogy from Jacques Derrida to Joseph Beuys*. Baltimore: Johns Hopkins UP, 1985.

2

Pedagogy: From the Periphery to the Center

Mariolina Salvatori

To believe in the poststructuralist axiom that to-read-is-to-write-is-to-read at more than a theoretical level, to extend, that is, in order to test its power, the rigorous enactment of that theory to the classroom—whatever the level of students' expertise, whatever the "field" of instruction—and if necessary to modify the theory in light of what classroom practice can teach, calls for a reassessment of what we mean by pedagogy. In the last ten years or so, in the teaching of literature as well as in the teaching of composition, the interconnections between the activities of reading and writing have been affirmed, explored, and exploited; entire curricula have been redesigned in the name of this axiom; yet not enough attention, I believe, has been paid to the radical questions that the enactment of this theory asks of our practice as teachers.

In this essay, I want to present, to put before us, two "scenes"—one in which teaching and learning are "framed" by a text-oriented theory and practice of reading, the other by a reader-oriented theory and practice of reading. In so doing, I hope to make "visible" some of the epistemological assumptions that inform the two "ways of reading" in order to uncover the radically different implications that such assumptions have for the teaching of reading and writing as *interrelated* activities.

My ultimate goal is to reclaim the value and the function of pedagogy by distinguishing it from didactics, a "subpart" of pedagogy that (for reasons I will be unable to articulate within the scope of this essay) has too often taken over, in the history of American education, indeed usurped, its domain.

Let me begin by providing yet another frame, a "polemical preamble" that is much more central to my whole argument than its preliminary location might suggest.

A Polemical Preamble

> We already know enough about methodology to do a good job of teaching reading and writing. Of course we would profit from knowing still more about teaching methods, but better teaching techniques alone would produce only a marginal improvement in the literacy of our students. Raising their reading and writing levels will depend far less on our methods of instruction (there are many acceptable methods) than on the specific contents of our school curricula.
>
> —E. D. Hirsch, Jr., "Cultural Literacy"

In *The Philosophy of Composition* Hirsch had advocated the separation of the teaching of literature (reading) from the teaching of composition (writing) arguing that collective ignorance about effective ways to teach composition had led composition teachers "to mix composition with other instructional goals" (140). One of the reasons he adduced for the advisability of such separation was the following:

> . . . it can be shown that knowing how to write is different from knowing about literature. The proof is simple. Numbers of graduate students in literature are unable to write well, yet they do demonstrably know a great deal about literature, much more than a freshman could possibly learn in a composition course. Whatever the theory may have been under which the teaching of literature was thought to be closely connected with writing skills, that theory has been shown to be incorrect by this simple empirical test. (141)

Insofar as the premise of Hirsch's argument was that knowing about literature was the only kind of knowing that teachers of literature can foster, and insofar as it is indisputable that "knowing how to write is different from knowing about literature," it could be argued that his call for the instructional separation of literature and composition was both a responsible and a justifiable act. "We know a lot more about literature than we know about teaching the craft of prose"—he declared—and citing the example of graduate students who "are unable to write well, yet . . . demonstrably know a great deal about literature" he intimated that what graduate students learn or do not learn is determined by what teachers know or do not know how to teach.

Assuming this to be the logic of the argument, let me point out that a different set of assumptions and expectations about the teaching and learning of reading would raise different questions (and lead to different conclusions) about what students' performance is a proof of. For example: what is the correlation between a theory of reading that produces "knowing about" and the understanding and the practice of reading and writing as unconnected, even divergent activities? And, might it not be advisable to modify (to retheorize) that theory in light of what classroom practice indicates?

True to the etymology of the word, a reading that produces knowing *about* suggests that the one who does the reading is positioned *outside, at a distance from* the text. While in the case of an (always already) expert reader, being outside, at a distance, may suggest a stance of objectivity, even the possibility of a wider, more encompassing perspective, in the case of a novice reader, such positioning suggests (always already) a negative distance that can only be "corrected" through the intervention of an expert who will provide, having acquired it from somebody else, the necessary information about the author, the text, the times it represents, its style, its meaning, and so forth. The kind of writing that this approach to reading has predominantly fostered is "writing about," a writing that distances even more the novice reader/writer from the text, and erects an impenetrable barrier between the reading and writing that has produced the author's text, and the student's reading and writing about it.

But let us imagine the act of reading as the opportunity for a reader to rethink, to retrace, and to ask, as Gadamer suggests, the questions that a text might be an answer to and the questions it might have silenced, as well as the opportunity to examine, to call into question, to modify both one's prejudgments about how/what one knows, and about how/what others know. This reading would require that the reader position himself or herself, simultaneously and recursively, both outside and within the text. And this positioning might make it possible for reading to be more fruitfully understood as a form of writing, and for it to be argued that learning to read *is* learning to write. I will return to this in part 2 of this essay.

Subsequently, Hirsch repudiated his earlier position (the instructional separation of literature and composition) claiming that "in [his] campaign against putting literature in the composition course [he] had overlooked the obvious truth that teaching literature can mean, when responsibly done, the teaching of *reading*. And it is inherently obvious that we cannot write better than we can read" ("Research in Writing: The Issues" 161–62).

However, the reversal of his position on the usefulness of teaching reading and writing together neither led to nor suggested the need for a critical investigation of which theory of reading (or which theory of writing) would justify and which would instead invalidate the possibility of teaching one activity through the other and of deepening the understanding of one through the understanding of the other. By accepting the relationship between reading and writing as an "obvious truth," as "inherently obvious," Hirsch reduced this relationship to a commonplace: "Some educators propose writing instruction as a good technique for reading instruction, and there is even reason to think that the opposite is also valid—valid enough, certainly, to cool down my earlier zeal and partisanship against teaching analytical reading in the writing class" (162).

In his continued concern with educational problems, Hirsch became involved in a long-term study of the correlations between writers' prior knowledge about the texts they are reading and writing about and the level of proficiency in their writing about them. He concluded that the more writers already know *about* the texts they are writing about the better their understanding of and writing *about* them. The solution he proposed was the teaching of background knowledge, which was to become the basis of his cultural literacy programme.

To what extent this prior knowing about a text differs from the "knowing about literature" demonstrated by the graduate students he refers to in *The Philosophy of Composition,* and why within the programme of cultural literacy this knowing should produce better writing is not ultimately clear.[1]

But what seems clear to me is that a teacher's adoption of a theory of reading that privileges and counts on prior background information can ultimately stifle a reader's involvement in reflexivity on the reading act and obliterate the understanding and the practice of reading and writing as interrelated, self-reflexive, and reciprocally illuminating activities.

As I bring this polemical preamble to a provisional closure, at the risk of stressing what some readers might already or by now find obvious, I want to go back to the passage from "Cultural Literacy" I have used as an epigraph in order to foreground the parts of Hirsch's statement that I feel compelled to question: the matter-of-fact way in which *now* reading and writing have become "complementary" activities (but how so?) although the approach to the teaching of reading does not seem to have been revised; his identification of teaching with "teaching techniques"; his intimating that literacy is not so much a matter of one's involvement in the activities of reading and writing as a matter of acquiring, of being given, a certain pre-scribed amount of knowledge; and above all, the simplistic view of pedagogy that his statement about methods of instruction can disseminate. "Raising their reading and writing levels will depend far less on our methods of instruction (there are many acceptable methods) than on the specific contents of our school curricula."[2] The fact that the remark, "there are many acceptable methods," is made parenthetically, is itself a telling gesture. On the one hand, it can be read as a generous gesture of pluralism; on the other hand, the generosity is contained, tucked away, between parentheses. Are there really many acceptable methods? Is it indeed possible to teach reading and writing as complementary, interrelated activities, no matter what a teacher's view of reading is?

Of course not. The way a teacher posits reading *does* matter and I will try to show why by presenting two scenes of instruction, one framed by a text-oriented theory of reading (of which Hirsch can be seen as a representative theorist and practitioner) the other framed by a reader-oriented theory of reading. My purpose is to analyze the potentialities for teaching, learning, and knowing that the two theories foster. The two "theories" which I offer as examples of irrec-oncilable methods are of course my interpretive constructs of two much more complex traditions. Since my focus is the kind of relation-ships that these theories make possible between readers and texts, students and teachers, this very focus will inevitably blur many other important features of these theories.

Part 1. A Text-oriented Theory of Reading

Here is an example of a text-oriented theory of reading: "But sometimes work is created of so resplendent a quality, so massive a solidity of imagination, that adverse criticism beats against it idly as the wind that flings its ineffectual force against a mountain-rock. Any profitable commentary on such work must necessarily tend towards a pure interpretation" (Wilson Knight, *The Wheel of Fire* 2). Knight's words, like the words of the author he writes about, William Shakespeare, *create;* they create the work as "icon" and warn that any reading that does not recognize it as such will be "iconoclastic," but only metaphorically so, since the work's "massive solidity" will withstand any attack.

This excerpt comes from the famous essay in which Knight sets up the distinction between "interpretation" and "criticism." The two terms, it seems to me, can function as metonyms for the two hierarchically differentiated reading practices that text-oriented theories of reading—whether formalist, structuralist, or "old" hermeneutical—inevitably seem to assign to expert and novice readers.[3]

Let me begin with "interpretation." Interpretation, Knight says,

> tends to merge into the work it analyses; it attempts, as far as possible, to understand its subject in the light of its own nature, employing external reference, if at all, only as preliminary to understanding; it avoids discussion of merits, and, since its existence depends entirely on an original acceptance of the validity of the poetic unit it claims, in some measure, to translate into discursive reasoning, it can recognize no division of "good" from "bad." . . . interpretation is passive, and looks back, regarding only the imperative challenge of poetic vision. . . . interpretation [is] a reconstruction of vision. (1–2)

But, he declares, "to receive the whole Shakespearean vision into the intellectual consciousness *demands a certain and very definite act of mind.* One must be prepared to see the whole play in space as well as in time" (3, emphasis added).

He then proceeds to map out the principles of interpretation — principles that have so much to do with matters of taste, sensibility, and affinity with the author's vision as to be ultimately unteachable. *Which is exactly the point I want to make.* In the pedagogical scene that is framed by and frames this way of reading, a critic like Knight constitutes himself as the "guardian," the "high priest" of the work-as-icon and as the intermediary of its "vision," and in so doing he issues forth a hierarchy of "controls" in between the work and the reader. What are some of the implications that this practice would have for teaching and learning? Well, let us imagine an undergraduate literature classroom, or a composition classroom . . . The student will gain access to the *sanctum sanctorum* of the literary work through the teacher who will "interpret" for him or her—that is, will "reconstruct," not criticize—Knight's translation of Shakespeare's vision/meaning.

This is a way of reading that aims at "preserving" the integrity, the mystery of the work of art. But it does so at the expense of the common, the noninitiated reader, who is constituted as the consumer of somebody's "reconstruction" of the original. The somebody who reconstructs the original constitutes himself or herself in the reconstruction as an other-father, an other-beginner, an other-begetter of a text that being so close to the original ought to inspire in its readers the same kind of veneration.

One of the problems of this veneration stance is that it disables the visionless reader from actually approaching the text. In this pedagogical scene, the secrecy of hermeneutics (rather, of this version of hermeneutics) not only sets up a hermetic circle that excludes the noninitiated; it also invalidates the possibility of entering in a dialogue with, of questioning, or formulating a critique of both the work and its guardian's account. What then is left for a student to write about but, in a gesture of "appreciation" that ultimately lacks authenticity, a panegyric on Shakespeare's "unique" contributions to world literature, or "vivid" use of imagery, or "powerful" psychological insights into human nature . . .

When a teacher unreflexively enacts for or with his or her students a theory of reading that focuses on the text as the manifestation of, the locus of, the writer's vision, that teacher will tend to valorize traditional concepts of authorship and authority.[4] This way of reading constitutes the writer as the Author, the Creator who creates out of the raw data of experience a "unique," inimitable, artifact. The author "lives" in his work, having inscribed himself in the text through the signature of his style; he also outlives his work if through it he attains the power or status granted to those who stand the test of time. Often praised in terms of being the "first," these works usually set up standards for subsequent writers. As objects of veneration, they are unapproachable except through the codified, ritualistic pilgrimage of exegesis that only those who already know its codifications and rituals can undertake.

Let me now move to Knight's definition of "criticism," and let me intimate, very briefly, the consequences of this way of reading for teaching and learning. Knight defines criticism, an activity he reserves for *lesser* works, as "the deliberate objectifying of the work under consideration; the comparison of it with other similar works in order especially to show in what respects it surpasses, or falls short of, those works; the dividing of its 'good' from its 'bad'; and, finally, a formal judgment as to its lasting validity" (1).

To the extent that its rules are made explicit, criticism, unlike interpretation, is teachable; but, it seems to me, it can only foster pseudolearning since what it teaches is to distinguish between the good, which is what readers endowed with vision can interpret, and the bad, which is what readers endowed with vision label as such and readers without vision learn to recognize.

The distinction between interpretation and criticism has as its analogues the distinction between literary texts and student texts, and the "readings" appropriate to both. And, I will claim, this distinction can be held responsible for according a different status to the teacher of literature and the teacher of composition, for underwriting the disciplinary separation between literature and composition, and for rendering the reading of literary texts in the composition classroom incongruous, indeed useless.

In my polemical preamble, I questioned, among other things, the accuracy of Hirsch's parenthetical remark, "there are many acceptable methods" to teach reading and writing together. Now I want to approach the inaccuracy from another angle.

Given his literary theory, the one he constructed in *Validity in Interpretation* and *The Aims of Interpretation,* E. D. Hirsch, Jr., cannot justify the use of any other method of reading, both in the composition and in the (undergraduate?) literature classroom, except the method that makes possible and is made possible by "cultural literacy": the reliance on and the "remedial" inculcation of prior background knowledge. Like Knight's distinction between interpretation and criticism, Hirsch's distinction between what he calls "primary interpretation" and "secondary interpretation," as we shall see, leads to hierarchical ways of reading and exclusionary pedagogical practices. The impossibility for reading and writing to be understood, practiced, and taught as interrelated activities within the programme of cultural literacy, in other words, has its origins in Hirsch's literary theory.

To argue this point, let me now move to another piece by Hirsch, the written version of a talk he delivered at the Center for the Humanities at Stanford University, which Graff and Gibbons, in *Criticism in the University,* have included in the section titled "Pedagogy and Polemics."

In "Back to History"—a title that functions both as an evaluation (i.e., there is nothing new under the sun) and an exhortation (let us go back to the past)—Hirsch names, "for simplicity" he claims, the split between Christopher Ricks and Frank Kermode—the split that disrupted the English Department of Cambridge University—the "Great Literary Theory Debate." This debate, he claims, is nothing but the resuscitation of the old debate between the Ancients and the Moderns. But in its "nontrivial form," Hirsch proposes, the current debate is

> ... about a practical matter: how should literature be taught and how should it be dealt with in our culture? On this "practical" question, the Ancients have this to say: the proper starting point for teaching the literature of the past is to recover its past meaning. . . . The Ancients view the literary texts that have come down to us as past speech acts which need to be understood as historical events. *They therefore believe that a teacher's first job is to help students recover the historical meaning* [emphasis added]. That was why they trained themselves as historical scholars—to keep alive in the present the meanings of the past. . . . Their aim of historical recovery could be called "primary interpretation."
>
> The Moderns, for their part, repudiate this historical approach, first of all on cultural grounds. Primary interpretation, they say, is a deadening enterprise. It turns the great works of literature into museum objects. . . . The real job of a teacher is to respeak, or revitalize, the texts of the past, and *make* them mean something to the present. The true aim of criticism is secondary interpretation, or what Foucalt calls "*resemanticizing* the text." (190)

In the rest of the essay, Hirsch continues to develop his parallel analysis, mainly in terms of irreconcilable differences; then, in support of his argument, he produces a letter written by an undergraduate to the *Times Literary Supplement* on the Great Literary Theory Debate. In this letter, an anonymous undergraduate complains that students were not invited to contribute an opinion on the crisis facing the teaching of English at Cambridge. The student regrets that "the interests of the student body as a whole were often forgotten" with the "honorable exception [of] Malcom Bradbury."

> The honorable exception was Malcom Bradbury who clearly has the students at heart when he suggests that

"many . . . come into English to engage with the humane
pleasure of particular books, and are not delighted to be
instructed in the modes of deconstruction of texts, of engaging a universalist narrative grammar, and of amassing
literary theory." For myself, as a recent graduate of Cambridge, I can only say that Bradbury's suggestion is entirely accurate. . . . (191)

Siding with the "undergraduates who want to study literature
. . . [who] want to discover the primary meanings of literature, and
engage in primary interpretation . . . who want to know what the
great authors meant, and why their works have been and still are
considered to be great. . . ." (191), Hirsch finally suggests that the
Great Literary Theory Debate is "the ideological manifestation of
an interest conflict" between professors and undergraduates. This
conflict of interest is "just the effect of a deeper institutional cause."
The "publish or perish" law has forced professors toward "the endless
frontier of secondary interpretation because they believe that the
frontier of primary, historical interpretation is closing down." He
goes on to say:

Each new reading of the "Tyger" by William Blake, if it
is significant and true, must decrease the chance that the
next reading can be significant and true—and new. So,
given the law of interpretation, and given the institutional
imperative to publish, professors have recently turned to
secondary creative interpretation, with its limitless frontier, to satisfy the institutional need for limitless publication. That is the source of the interest conflict between
professors and undergraduates. Both parties are caught
up in the vortex of institutional homeostasis, i.e., the instinct of the academy, like any other institution, to maintain itself as it is—no matter how adversely this homeostasis affects the educational purposes of the academy. (192–
93)

By reducing the conflict to a clash of interest, by suggesting that
current theories of reading are a response to the institutional demand
for publications, Hirsch singlehandedly dismisses (and prevents himself from reflecting on) the valuable theoretical insights that poststructuralists have provided—insights that have greatly contributed
to transforming the practice of many readers, writers, and teachers

in the last two decades. (Perhaps a History of Pedagogy, which we do not have yet, might make this clear.) Back to History, indeed. And the fact that *that* history, his version of history, may have been responsible for separating the teaching of reading from the teaching of writing, the discipline of composition from the discipline of litera-ture, is a realization that his theory of reading cannot engender.

If Hirsch *really* believed that there are other acceptable methods to teach reading, he would also have to entertain the possibility that readers perform "secondary interpretations" for reasons other than the surplus of already available primary interpretations (a surplus, by the way, that negates the possibility that graduate students and younger critics can perform "primary interpretations"). If he really were to confront the implications of what he is saying, his concept of cultural literacy would have to be retheorized, and the institutional practices that both are supported by and support it would have to be modified.

Part 2. A Reader-oriented Theory of Reading

> Once a text is credited with high authority it is studied in-
> tensely; once it is so studied it acquires mystery or secrecy.
> —Frank Kermode, *The Genesis of Secrecy*

A theory of reading that focuses on a text's "genesis of secrecy" or "mystery" and in so doing discovers (uncovers) the role of the reader as a "performer" of a script, or a "collaborator" in the production of the work, or a "maker of a meaning" or of meanings that a text only suggests, or as an "interlocutor," has the potential to call into question, or at least to interrogate, the traditional concept of a writ-er's/text's authorship and authority. As long as this calling into question, this interrogation, is not just a game through which a teacher ultimately appropriates, assumes, the authority and author-ship he or she subtracts from authors and texts, the configuration of the teaching and learning context undergoes radical changes.

During the 1960s and 1970s, partly as a revolt against the excessive strictures of the techniques of formalism, and against the structural-ists' separation of poetic theory from interpretive practice, partly, I would like to believe, as an interrogation of the paradoxical gesture of educators whose professional expertise was ultimately to erode the confidence of anybody who was not a literature major ever appro-priately to understand a literary text, literary criticism began to raise explicit and pertinent questions about the role of the reader in the reading process. In various ways, for various reasons, theoretical and practical criticism began to ask what at first seemed (and to some still seem) incongruous and irreverent questions: what do readers do and how they do what they do when they read a text, and what is it they read when they read? One of the most immediate and lasting consequences of this approach is that traditional assumptions about a writer's/text's authority are either called into question or are at least reexamined in terms of how readers constitute them in the act of reading. To read, to perceive an author's work as the progressive perfecting of an intention, rather than an intention perfected, realized, achieved, calls into question the myth that works are "fathered" by an inexplicable fiat; to read a text in order to examine, to reconstruct the process, the work *in fieri*, calls attention to the experienced writer's successive phases of evolution and discovery, and makes it possible for a teacher to read an inexperienced writer's writing, and to teach him or her how to read it, as a manifestation of similar struggles with language. Student writing can then be seen as an instantiation of creativity, and as a subject worthy of study and research. And a teacher's reading of student writing can be seen as an activity that, to say the least, demands intensity of study, critical training, challenging questionings equal to the ones typically reserved for the reading of those texts that the politics of our profession anoints as status-granting.

Divorced from its phenomenological and philosophical antecedents, this approach to reading has come to be known in this country by the problematic denomination of "reader-response" theory and criticism.[5] At their best, theorists and practitioners of reader-response have produced a keen awareness of a critic/reader's responsibility to construct, to reflect on, and to account for, his or her interpretation of a text. At their worst, they have produced and encouraged readings that have celebrated subjectivity and the rule-making activity and authority of a small enclave of readers. It is not my intention here to provide a critique of the movement. Jane Tompkins, Mary Louise Pratt, William Ray, Elizabeth Freund, among others, have provided intelligent critical readings of the aberrations of the movement. But what I want to suggest is that, in spite of its various and crucial limitations, this movement, seen as a response to the increasing awareness of the lack of self-examination that characterizes reductive applications of past methodological procedures, has had a considerable beneficial effect on the practice of teaching—the teaching of reading and the teaching of writing, and especially, the teaching of reading and writing as interrelated, inseparable activities.

This is not to say that reader-response theories *make* good teachers. To assume this implies that teachers are merely the applicators, the conveyors of somebody else's theories, themselves incapable to theorize, to interpret theories, to test and transform them, or it implies that theories must either "fit" the classroom, or otherwise be rejected. This is to suggest instead that the reflexivity, the turn inward, the interpellation of one's way of thinking/knowing—as one is confronted with another's way of thinking/knowing—that reader-response theories propose, can foster a more immediate, concrete understanding of and respect for social, collaborative, and cooperative rather than genial, mysterious, and hermetic constructions of knowledge.

Reader-response theorists purport to focus on the activity of readers reading in the reading process. It can be argued, however, that with a few exceptions (Richards, Holland, Bleich), most of the reader-response theorists who offer useful insights into the interrelatedness of reading and writing examine, and thus valorize, readers and texts that are marked by Authorship/Authority. Although this is a problem that can perpetuate the same institutional and disciplinary divisions that text-oriented theories of reading have created, this problem, I believe, can best be addressed, and resolved, from within the very contexts—the composition classroom, the undergraduate literature classroom, the "remedial" classroom—that some reader-oriented theories tend to exclude. These contexts, these scenes of instruction, make it imperative that we test, expand, modify, retheorize these theories. When by deconstructing the very theory we are using, by exposing that theory's blindness to its own gaps, its own absences, we make "the reader" mean also readers in the classroom, students, rather than the "implied" reader, or the "optimal" reader, the "super" reader, we place students' work, students' mental processes, students' texts center stage at the scene of instruction.[6]

Unless a teacher only pays lip service to this methodology, his or her hermeneutical activity will shift focus: from the literary text, to the text that represents the student's attempt at reading the literary text, at making it mean. "Inquiry," then, is no longer something that a critic, a teacher does *for* inexperienced readers/students. Inquiry becomes a rigorously structured collaborative activity that acknowledges as it relies on the student's productive abilities, and that calls for a visible, structural change in the realignment of the teacher/student interaction: the seminar type of arrangement, the tutoring session, the workshop. This interaction is made possible by and makes possible the recognition of a student's work as a form of knowledge in the process of formation. This interaction makes it possible for student and teacher to get to know each other, and to recognize each other as more than instantiations of roles.

The teaching and learning context that is framed by and frames this view of reading calls for an epistemological script the performing of which can have liberating effects on its participants—students and teachers. When students are put in the position to ask questions of texts that foster the unfolding, rather than the concealing, of the drama of knowing—with all its uncertainties, obstacles, anxieties, resolutions, complications—as that drama is either recorded in authors' texts or in professional critics' attempts to account for the genesis of those texts—students may recognize in those texts manifestations of their own dramas and might consequently come to understand and accept the reasons for their own anxiety about or defense against knowing.

And teachers may learn to re-cognize, may learn to relearn, their own clumsy, uncertain beginnings as makers of meanings; teachers may learn to re-member, that is to put together again, the steps they took to pull themselves out of confusion, and use that memory to begin again the inquiry into how, into what one knows and can know with their students, at the place where the students are.

Looking Back, Looking Ahead

The difference between the ways text-oriented and reader-oriented theories of reading define authority and authorship has profound implications for teaching and learning and for the role that teachers and students can claim in the production of knowledge. More specifically, a text-oriented theory of reading is not conducive to teaching reading and writing as interrelated activities. Neither is it conducive to the approach to the teaching of writing that has so drastically transformed the discipline of composition in the last ten or fifteen years.

I would like to conclude this essay by proposing that the first scene I have construed be defined as the domain of didactics, and that the second be defined as the domain of pedagogy.

Because I want to reclaim pedagogy as a "philosophical science," as a theory and practice of knowing that makes manifest its own theory and practice by continuously reflecting on, deconstructing, and getting to know one's theory and practice, I suggest we call didactics that concept of teaching and learning—in whatever discipline—that programmatically invalidates teachers' and students' critical reflexivity on the act of knowing, and promotes the reduction of somebody else's method of knowing into a sequential schematization of that method.

Didactics sets up models and dictates procedures that claim to make the approximation of those models possible; pedagogy, on the other hand, inquires into the prehistory of those models, and analyzes and assesses their formation.[7] The radically different epistemological assumptions at the basis of didactics and pedagogy, as I hope to have demonstrated in my analysis of the two teaching and learning contexts, determine radically different teacher/learner relationships, classroom activities, projects, curricula. To recognize these differences might help understand and guard against the reasons for the incongruous, the unforgivable, the unjustifiable professional and institutional marginalization of pedagogy in American education.

Although for rhetorical purposes I have posed, as the antagonists, Wilson Knight, E. D. Hirsch, Jr., and the hypothetical teacher who unreflexively utilizes a text-oriented theory of reading to institute, whether consciously or unconsciously, a hierarchy of power, it is ultimately the dogmatic part of myself I recognize in them that I am so passionately arguing with. As I observe and think through my own practice, and the practice of my students, of graduate students and colleagues, of theorists and teachers whose work I read, I discover, over and over again, that "the dogmatic persona" haunts most of us and keeps intruding on the scene as a cover-up for insecurity, intransigence, faulty logic, or sheer tiredness. This persona, I believe, can be more effectively kept under scrutiny when both as theorists and teachers we learn to conceptualize pedagogy as more than "teaching methods," "teaching techniques"; when, that is, we bring pedagogy from the periphery to the center of our profession.

Notes

1. In a recent review of *Cultural Literacy,* Robert Scholes argues that the problem Hirsch describes is real but that the "solution proposed is both absurd in itself and eerily disconnected from the material Hirsch presents to support it. Hirsch's treatment of this supporting evidence needs extensive examination . . ." (328). In a similar vein, in " 'Cultural Literacy': A Critical Reading," I have

argued for the need to pay attention to Hirsch's logic. In this essay I reproduce and expand on that argument, as I began to address it in "Reading and Writing a Text" and in the essay published in *Correspondences*.

2. The call to English teachers to assume their responsibility as educators, that is, to reclaim the "acculturative tradition," the emphasis on their "duty," and on the "mission of 'English' " are recurrent themes in Hirsch's work. As admirable as his commitment and aspirations are, it must be pointed out, however, how both his commitment and aspirations lead him to deemphasize the duty and the responsibility of the student in the learning process and to assign to the teacher, instead, the major if not the sole responsibility for the production of knowledge. For a critique of this approach to knowing, see John Warnock, "Cultural Literacy: A Worm in the Bud?"

3. Knight is extremely careful to clarify that his remarks are not prescriptive and that his distinction is less rigid than it seems: "[i]n practice, it is probable that neither can exist, or at least has yet on any comprehensive scale existed, quite divorced from the other" (2). Let me declare my respect for his work, and for his respect for Shakespeare. I do not intend to be iconoclastic. My intent is to unravel the implications that an uncritical, unreflexive application of his veneration stance (a veneration stance that in his case is borne not of ignorance, but of knowledge, although of a knowledge that seems to be the province of the elect) can have for teaching and learning. In this essay I am using Knight, and Hirsch, to frame my discussion of pedagogy.

4. Michel Foucault (See *The Archeology of Knowledge* and *Language, Counter-Memory, Practice*) and Edward W. Said (*Beginnings* and *The World, the Text, and the Critic*) provide forceful critiques of traditional approaches to authorship, authority, text. For the implications that a revised understanding of these concepts can have for teaching and learning, see Sharon Crowley's "writing and Writing."

5. I use the term *reader-response* loosely to include those theories that, in Elizabeth Freund's words, attempt "to make the imperceptible process of reading perceptible by seeking to reopen to scrutiny that which has been declared inscrutable, illegitimate, or trivial" (5). Therefore I include in this field phenomenologists, new hermeneuticists (like Gadamer, Ricoeur, Kermode), sociologists of reading, reception theorists—theorists, in other words, who in various ways and to varying degrees examine and foster reflexivity on the complex transaction of knowledge that reading is.

6. I have already proposed the differences between pedagogy and

didactics in "Towards a Hermeneutics of Difficulty." I derive the articulation of this distinction from Giovanni Gentile, the Italian philosopher/educator contemporary of Benedetto Croce, who like other Continental philosophers, considered and practiced pedagogy as a "philosophical science."

7. For some examples of pedagogy see: David Bartholomae, "Inventing the University" and "Wanderings: Misreadings, Miswritings, Misunderstandings"; Patricia Donahue and Ellen Quandahl, "Freud and the Teaching of Interpretation"; Elizabeth Flynn, "Gender and Reading"; Thomas Newkirk, "Looking for Trouble: A Way to Unmask Our Readings"; Mariolina Salvatori, "Reading and Writing a Text: Correlations between Reading and Writing Patterns" and "Toward a Hermeneutics of Difficulty"; *Facts, Artifacts and Counterfacts,* ed. David Bartholomae and Anthony Petrosky.

Works Cited

Bartholomae, David. "Inventing the University." *When a Writer Can't Write.* Ed. Mike Rose. New York: Guilford, 1985. 134–65.

――――. "Wanderings: Misreadings, Misgivings, Misunderstandings." *Only Connect: Uniting Reading and Writing.* Ed. Thomas Newkirk. Upper Montclair, NJ: Boynton, 1986. 119–30.

Bartholomae, David, and Anthony Petrosky. eds. *Facts, Artifacts, and Counterfacts: Theory and Method for a Reading and Writing Course.* Upper Montclair, NJ: Boynton, 1986.

Crowley, Sharon. "writing and Writing." *Writing and Reading Differently: Deconstruction and the Teaching of Composition and Literature.* Ed. G. Douglas Atkins and Michael Johnson. Lawrence, Kansas: Kansas UP, 1985. 93–100.

Donahue, Patricia, and Ellen Quandahl. "Freud and the Teaching of Interpretation." *College English* 49.6 (Oct. 1987): 641–49.

Flynn, Elizabeth A. "Gender and Reading." *Gender and Reading: Essays on Readers, Texts, and Contexts.* Ed. Elizabeth A. Flynn and Patrocinio Schweickardt. Baltimore: Johns Hopkins UP, 1986. 267–88.

Foucault, Michel. *The Archeology of Knowledge.* Trans. A. M. Sheridan Smith. New York: Pantheon, 1972.

――――. *Language, Counter-Memory, Practice.* Ed. Donald F. Bouchard. Ithaca, NY: Cornell UP, 1977.

Freund, Elizabeth. *The Return of the Reader: Reader-Response Criticism*. New York: Methuen, 1987.

Gentile, Giovanni. *Sommario di Pedagogia come Scienza Filosofica*. 2 vols. Florence: Sansoni, 1982.

Hirsch, E. D., Jr. *The Aims of Interpretation*. Chicago: U of Chicago P, 1976.

———. "Back to History." *Criticism in the University*. Ed. Gerald Graff and Reginald Gibbons. Evanston, Il: Northwestern UP, 1985. 185–97.

———. "Cultural Literacy." *American Scholar* 52.2 (1983): 159–69.

———. *The Philosophy of Composition*. Chicago: U of Chicago P, 1977.

———. "Research in Writing: The Issues." *Basic Writing*. Ed. Lawrence N. Kasden and Daniel R. Hoeber. Urbana: NCTE, 1980. 153–63.

———. *Validity in Interpretation*. New Haven: Yale UP, 1967.

Kermode, Frank. *The Genesis of Secrecy: On the Interpretation of Narrative*. Cambridge: Harvard UP, 1979.

Knight, Wilson. *The Wheel of Fire*. London: Methuen, 1930.

Newkirk, Thomas. "Looking for Trouble: A Way to Unmask Our Readings." *College English* 46 (1984): 756–66.

Said, Edward. *Beginnings: Intention and Method*. Baltimore: Johns Hopkins UP, 1975.

———. *The World, the Text, the Critic*. Cambridge: Harvard UP, 1982.

Salvatori, Mariolina. " 'Cultural Literacy': A Critical Reading." *Correspondences Seven*. Ed. Ann E. Berthoff. Upper Montclair, NJ: Boynton, n.d.

———. "Reading and Writing a Text: Correlations between Reading and Writing Patterns." *College English* 45 (1983): 657–66.

———. "Towards a Hermeneutics of Difficulty." *Audits of Meaning*. Ed. Louise Z. Smith. Upper Montclair, NJ: Boynton, 1989. 80–95.

Scholes, Robert. "Three Views of Education: Nostalgia, History, and Voodoo." *College English* 50 (1988): 323–32.

Warnock, John. "Cultural Literacy: A Worm in the Bud?" *ADE Bulletin* 92 (1985): 1–7.

3

Interpretation and Betrayal: Talking with Authority

Dennis A. Foster

Most of the writing that students do at universities requires them to respond in some way to figures of authority. Because experiential knowledge is necessarily limited, we all must depend on textual authorities as bases for understanding and education: independent, original knowledge is little more than an appealing fiction for most, if not all, of us. Consequently, critical writing demands that authorities be interpreted, analyzed, quoted, questioned, and so forth. But given this situation, the goals of a university, what has been called a liberal education, present a troubling paradox for most students, a double bind: they must at once respect and resist authority, be "good students" and independent thinkers, imitators and originals. Cardinal Newman's statement on the role of the university still applies to contemporary universities, despite the technological turn our culture has taken: they are responsible for a product, the good citizen of democratic societies, a paradoxical blend of conformity and independent thought embodied in the "good" (i.e., both obedient and questioning) student. The relation of writing to authority that students learn at the university, I am suggesting, can define for them a position within society.

Writing on pedagogy, Shoshana Felman has argued that thinking "is always both motivated and obscured by love" (Felman 35). The writers and writings that most preoccupy us, from which we learn the most, often have the power to produce feelings of trust and desire akin to this complicating love. The need to understand, to find some secure position of control and mastery leads us to identify certain, often peculiarly chosen, texts as sources of knowledge. Not surprisingly, the insights passionate reading leads to always occur at the cost of a certain blindness, a limitation that need not devalue the significance of the insights. Blindness is a necessary part of the process. The inability most people eventually feel to make commitments to new "texts" may, in fact, mark the limits of their ability to learn something new. We must abandon some point of certainty to accept new figures of truth.[1]

The bearers of these new figures resemble a psychological entity Jacques Lacan calls the Subject Supposed to Know. Within the psychoanalytic situation, the analyst comes to stand for the S.s.S. (as Lacan tellingly abbreviates), the subject the analysand looks to as the one who will be able to make sense of a confused life's story. The analyst is supposed to be able to confirm or deny the truth of the analysand's words and restore a lost certainty. In fact, however, the analyst is never the actual source of truth. Rather, the Subject Supposed to Know represents an imaginary position that can be filled variously thoughout one's life by a succession of figures modeled in some way on a lost image of authority from childhood, of a mother or father imagined to be all-powerful.[2] This modeling is what psychoanalysis calls transference. For Lacan, transference is not limited to the relation between a psychoanalyst and a patient, but occurs whenever the love that was learned in childhood is transfered onto another figure; and wherever transference occurs, there is a Subject Supposed to Know. In other words, we produce our authorities when we see them through the eyes of our past, transforming the actual, whether it is brilliant or dull, into an image of an earlier object of love and trust.

Interpretation is largely motivated by this faith in an authority based on the repetition of what was originally an illusion, a projection onto a parental figure. Believing in writers makes the pursuit of their knowledge seem worthwhile, a goal both meaningful and attainable. Interpretation, that is, is a kind of love. So long as we read with love, we ask questions of authority believing that we will be answered, that some great soul, such as James' Vereker in "The Figure in the Carpet," will clasp us to his or her confirming bosom. It is hard to imagine the real labor of interpretation proceding without such a promise.

This productive relationship is troubled, however, by the promise's being false. Someone may emerge to reassure us, to keep us from recognizing the pattern of repetition, but no one has the authority of final truths. Authority in the sense I have been using it is a manifestation of the Lacanian Phallic: that is, it is a delusion, a consequence of a *méconnaissance,* a misrecognition in childhood that leads us to perceive that which we need to survive (a parent) as a kind of god. The loss of this parental divinity leaves us with a lasting need to find a substitute for that phallic authority, to imitate it, to make it our own. Juliet Mitchell, seeing the pathos of this dilemma, identifies the insoluble problem of the masculine to be the desire to represent the phallus.[3] I would broaden this formulation to include both sexes, saying that all desire for authority leads to imperson-ation, to playing the Man that Style makes. What this implies is that between Authority and the limited knowledge of a real world is a gap that is covered over by love.

The problem for university students in responding to authority is complicated by the fact that the speakers and writers they come in contact with have dedicated much of their lives to perfecting the impersonation of authority as a necessary prerequisite to being heard. And writers are assisted in their disguise by teachers who encourage, even require, a kind of belief in the "classics," the mas-ters, the great originals (i.e., "fine writing") as if fearing that a lack of respect for authority will leave students skeptical and scornful of their betters. Even the so-called "hermeneutics of suspicion," so reviled by humanists, is no escape from this dilemma but only a shifting of allegiance to the authorities of Freud and Marx, for exam-ple. Yet if "suspicion" is not an answer, how can one move beyond the initially motivating, but ultimately obscuring power of transference?

The concept of suspicion implies that one must carefully watch the pronouncements of authorities because they might try to pass falsehood for truth—as if telling the truth were a real alternative. But Jane Gallop writes of a Lacanian strategy that avoids the either/or of suspicion. If transference involves the enamoured reader in the attempt to speak in the language of the Subject Supposed to Know, to transfer, carry across, knowledge to oneself, then translation (de-rived from the past participle of the root of transference) is the completed transference, the realization of that knowledge in the reader's own tongue (Gallop 52). That difficult knowledge that had been desired in another is made one's own, different certainly from its authoritative form, debased even, some would say, as they might say all translations are less than the original. Translations, insofar as they are literally misrepresentations, are a form of traducing.

To make the metaphor even more explicit, the love that inspires interpretation leads eventually to betrayal.

The emotionally charged terms I am using speak to the genuine struggle readers feel as they separate themselves through interpretation from the position of absolute faith in a beloved authority. When the passion of transference passes, it is hard to look at the difference between the actual writer and the semidivine figure love had imagined without either resenting the actual or denying the vision. But such a process must be experienced if one is not to read always in subservience, conscious or not, to an imaginary master.

Plato, Augustine, Pope, and other masters have dictated a proper reading to be one that adheres to the spirit of the text. Without being quite an argument for authorial intention, such commands to the reader have assumed the presence of a truth that might be approached through an inadequate language, a prior truth that had been revealed to the writer. The history of rhetoric has been the development and analysis of styles of authority that produce such readings. If writers would be persuasive, would be believed, they need to create readers who are willing to have some faith in them. Clearly, such a relation between writers and readers is necessary at certain periods for learning to take place, but it is also a limiting, even ultimately stunting relation. Lacan suggests how we might move past that point.

The Lacanian strategy implies a shift of attention from the spirit to the letter. Lacan's essay, "The agency of the letter in the unconscious," demonstrates the power of the "letter," the part displaced from the context of the larger Word to another context, to produce powerful effects at variance with the "spirit" of the whole.[4] The supposition of wholeness in a text constitutes the impenetrable face of authority. If a denial of that wholeness through a reading of the letter is not seen simply as a betrayal of the spirit, but as an acknowledgement of what a writer has in fact produced, we can begin to respond to the "literal" power of writing.

This project may seem beside the point in a time when the average university student reads so little as not to be limited by a love for any writing. But what links the first-year nonreader and those who read for spirit is the faith they share in authority and a disregard for the letter, for the material details of life that must be read even to be seen. The initial problem, however, is to place students in situations where they can begin to recognize the power that writing has always exerted in their world. Only then can they begin to realize that writing itself exists as an area where they might resist authority, and that the effects of authority can be reproduced in their own writing. The rest of this essay will present three brief expositions on how the insights of a Lacanian analysis can enter a course in composition.

At some point, most of us spend time teaching deductive logic, either as a method of producing and analyzing arguments, or as a rhetorical tactic. The importance of teaching some basic principles of formal logic has only partly to do with logic's power to produce "valid" statements, however. In fact, it is quite rare that a really valid syllogism appears in prose. However, the general form of deductive logic carries a heavy emotional weight in Western culture: deduction is the sign of truth, even more than being its method. It is a constituent element of the "Subject Supposed to Know," the voice that ensures readers they have a connection with the truth. Consequently, few arguments can hope to prevail that do not *sound* logical, whether they are or not. In the midst of a course where students are continually baffled by that elusive quality *clarity,* logic comes, if well taught, as a moment of amazing certainty: at last, someone knows the truth! It also brings the high merriment of discovering fallacies, with the delicious sense that anyone can detect falsehood once he or she has seen the shape of truth. Never mind that students cannot themselves produce meaningful syllogisms as a part of their arguments, can seldom actually ferret out the fallacies or reconstruct the enthymemes in any professionally written essay. This stage of insight and possibility nevertheless suggests a purposiveness to analytic thought. But the teaching of logic is curative in another way: it comes as a sort of inoculation, as a virus that, at least temporarily, can transform the apparent chaos of thought into replications of its own form. And in experiencing this fever of certainty, one can learn to recognize and hence become immune to (or at least skeptical of) the sign of truth in logic.

This is not to undervalue deductive logic and the real accomplishments it has made possible for Western culture, but to avoid overvaluing it. Its inability to deal with what it must see as paradox or ambiguity does not deny its utility in its proper fields. The fact that deductive logic is ultimately grounded in intuition, metaphor, "inductive experience," tautology, and so forth, does not invalidate it, but rightly separates it from the realm of absolute truth. Our students should be able to make this separation or they will remain subject to the confusion of logic-as-formal-questioning with logic-as-truth, a confusion that gives the discourse of logic its tremendous currency in ordinary language, whether it appears in the careful constructions of intellectuals or in the smooth parodies in sales and politics. The work in class would need to move the students initially through the forms of logic, getting them to produce their own syllogisms and to abstract them (both the valid and the fallacious) from the writing of others. They need to develop a feel for the formal argument that underlies the discursive prose, for only then will it make sense to them that this feeling might be the product as much of style as of logical structure. After this classroom work, the process of teaching them to analyze the specific ways in which the tone of rational argument is achieved would require a series of assignments, taking them through love and betrayal, toward something like wisdom. I would begin with an analysis of the logic of an argumentative essay, looking to see why it is persuasive, how it makes its case. Many of the essays in a good reader provide examples with which I might work. The point at this stage is to get students to sense and admire the power of a well-written essay, whether or not they agree with the thesis. Most experienced readers, for example, admire the clear, reasonable tone that Orwell attains in "Politics and the English Language," in spite of the fallacies and prejudices that a careful analysis will disclose. Such flaws in logic's facade are ultimately beside the point: few arguments are ever refuted by revelation of their fallacies; few succeed by their rigor. Nevertheless, in order to respond critically and effectively to an argument, students, inexperienced readers, must become sensitized to the discourse of logic, recognize it with the immediacy that we detect the features of old lovers in new faces. For unless we recognize it as a trope, device, or style that passes itself off as plain reason and common sense, we remain susceptible to the simple seduction of repetition, of the transference onto the limited present of an idea of logic that once promised truth.

My argument here is that in order to resist the authority of well-formulated arguments, to see, that is, both what is useful and what is illusory, we need first to recognize and then violate the sense of wholeness produced by the paradigm of "rationality." To achieve these ends, assignments might take the following design, one that the two subsequent examples will make concrete. The first assignment would ask students to read the argument "on its own terms," in its spirit, paraphrasing and elucidating its logic and implications. In the course of working through the argument, students would have a chance to look at the pieces that constitute an argument, a necessary step to the second stage of analysis. At that point, the assignment should ask students to resist the terms of the logic through an examination of inductive bases, implied categories, metaphors, and paradoxes. It is here that the specifically linguistic nature of argumentative logic can be addressed. The categories of language have neither the authority of nature nor the tautological certainty of mathematics: they are culturally determined and fit into the syllogistic structure only through our failure or refusal to question the terms. The point here is not to destroy the argument, but to see what else might be said: while Orwell's point about the connections between politics and language are laudable, his politics (his elitism, his resistance to innovation, his occasional xenophobia) deserves some further analysis. But it is precisely these less laudable, perhaps unintended, elements of his political language that open his essay to further discussion. What, for example, is the connection between his liberal politics and his desire for a linguistic purity with its implications of cultural elitism? The third stage might produce a supplementary interpretation of the text based on these questions, on what was screened from view by the governing logic of the piece. The fact that writers say something more than or different from what they apparently intend is not a failure, but an opening that allows readers to discover what they themselves have to say. Not every student will find the same openings in a text, and the kind of opening an analysis produces reveals something about the student reading. This third stage is where students can, through their own participation in the production of meaning, find out something about their relationship to social authority. And they should have learned about the provisional and fictive nature of authority, that it is something *produced* by writing.[5]

An example dealing with a relatively simple text may clarify this process. In 1973 Marabel Morgan published the highly successful book *The Total Woman*. Its success makes it an interesting text for my purpose because of the authority it assumed with many women in the 1970s. Its seeming transparency and its dated feel, on the other hand, open it to a ready analysis. I have frequently given the chapter "Admire Him" to first-year students—to their amazement. Briefly, the chapter advises that woman can make men into the confident and loving companions they want by "filling" a man's "empty cup" with admiration, whether or not admiration would seem his due. After the first moments of hilarity have died down, we reconstruct the political context of the book within the intense feminism of the early 1970s, and the students begin to take it seriously, to recognize first their own parents, and then to see their peers in the book. The first assignment asks them to respect the frustrations and desires of the women the book addresses and to explicate the advice and its reasoning, providing contemporary examples to supplement Morgan's argument: For example, what sort of lives do their mothers lead? How do fraternities and sororities interact? What kind of conversations do male and female students actually have? (Not surprisingly, women do better with this aspect of the assignment.) The purpose of the assignment is to get the students involved with the argument and to feel the quite real power Morgan's writing has. They should notice the kinds of authorities she invokes—the Bible, doctors—and explicate the homey directness of the cookery metaphors she employs. They should appreciate the real frustrations felt by women committed to the conventional lives of housewives. Ideally, I would like to see them looking to Morgan in hope, or fear, that she might indeed have an answer, might be the one supposed to know, though only a few students of the eighties will go so far with Morgan. But some such interest in Morgan's opinions, doctrines even, is important to a further understanding of how her writing works.

The second assignment asks for a careful textual analysis that overlooks the larger argument to focus on metaphors such as the "empty cup" that is man, on the various uses of the word *power*, on the specific representations of men, on the ways in which the authorities of doctors and the Bible are invoked. Invariably, students find ways in which the particulars, when focused on, fail to support the argument or suggest qualities possessed by both men and women that are unpleasant to consider. Women are depicted as manipulative, deceitful, and power-hungry victims, unaccountably drawn to their egotistical, childish, impotent, and otherwise loathsome men. These and other insights are not in opposition to Morgan's larger argument, but are the paradoxical excesses of her writing. Her desire to help women contains something dominating, cruel, and exploitative. When we focus on the letter of the text, a betrayal appears, though it is unclear whether it is a betrayal by an ungrateful reader who refuses Morgan's gift, or a betrayal by Morgan who plays on the pain of her readers. As Morgan's language is translated into the student's own, the gap between her "intention" and their reading begins to emerge.

The final assignment, and the only formal essay, asks the students to develop the implications of the second assignment, to make Morgan show her hand. Morgan's assumptions about the desire of women (for power before romance), her estimation of men (impotent, emotionally dead, literally empty until filled by women), and other such sad truths allow the students to generate rationales for the effectiveness of Morgan's book other than the initial hope that she provided answers to troubled women. Students begin to read tales that, had they not been screened by her primary "logic," would not have been acceptable to Morgan's original audience. Yet Morgan's insights (perhaps unconscious) into the apparently paradoxical dynamics of sexual relationships become valuable once more to my students as they translate them into their own tongue, if only because they can see motivations that are generally denied. They become able to think with something like independence about this issue by working through the ideological positions expressed in Morgan's doctrines and then seeing beyond their totalizing closure. This exercise should enable them to begin to perceive the contemporary *doxa* of under-graduates—that problems of sex and gender have been solved—and open it to question. It is not answers, but the ability to think without conclusions that emerges from this labor.

A more important and more problematically political text for most first-year students is *The Communist Manifesto*. The authority this book exerts in our world is a mystery to them, partly because they have not read it, but more because the book is too highly charged. American and British editors of the text generally attempt to cancel that charge through a discussion of the many failures of Marx's program and predictions, which leads students to evade the book rather than discover something of its power.[6] I am not going to attempt a reading of the book here, but only to provide a brief example of how a series of writing assignments might allow writing students to respond to the evident authority of Marx.

My ultimate purpose in this task is to let my students see that by writing about this troubling text they can understand something of its value without becoming "Marxists," whatever they think that means. My focus is narrow, getting them to read at least a few pages closely, to learn tactics of mastery rather than to master a particular a text. I generally choose the two pages early in the first chapter containing the anaphoric series of paragraphs each beginning with "The bourgeoisie." But before we turn attention there, I make the book seem familiar. As with Morgan's book, they need to know something of the history of mid-nineteenth-century industrial condi-tions, of the revolutions between 1776 and 1848, of Marx's own situation in exile. And then we read the list of measures Marx and Engels propose as necessary at the end of the second chapter, noting how many of them (abolition of child labor, graduated income tax, etc.) have been adopted in the United States. We recall our own Wobblies and the socialist impulses of the New Deal. Of course the abolition of private property remains problematic for them, but the point is to let them see the ordinary in what is at first apparently alien.

The passage we then concentrate on makes a series of claims about bourgeois, capitalist society, emphasizing the total subservience of all noble and idealistic impulses to the demands of capital, the "cash nexus." If our introductory discussion has overcome the sense of dangerous unfamiliarity in Marx, this notion that the world is organized through capital has an appeal nearly as galvanizing as that of logic. The cleanly reasonable form is so immediately applicable that most students are willing (for the experimental moment of class) to bracket their ideals to test the claim. Paternalism, chivalry, sentimentality, and nobility of lawyers, and so forth, these provide relatively simple objects for a Marxist analysis. The first assignment, then, is to explicate one or two paragraphs, filling out the examples Marx mentions and extending the thesis into a contemporary example. The purpose is to make the students provisional advocates of Marx so that they can demonstrate to themselves Marx's power and recognize the capacity of his model for interpreting certain economic and social relations. The limitations of such readings are less important than the appeal they can have in offering a new *doxa,* a doctrine to respond to problems the innocent reader may not have been aware existed the week before. Marx can be the one supposed to know.

The second assignment is again an analysis of fragments to discover something about how the argument is assembled. They might notice that it is not communists but the bourgeoisie that have "torn asunder" veils, have "stripped" off halos, "disclosed" brutalities, and thereby revealed so many bitter things about human motivations and relations. The bourgeoisie are the "most revolutionary" people in history, who transformed the world, who are the engine (if also the future victims) of revolution. Students might also see that the tone and content (the talk of "veils" and violence) of the passage would hardly be out of place in a church, or that the apocalyptic vision of revolution is borrowed from Christianity. They might hear the echoes of Shakespeare's Prospero in Marx's "all that is solid melts into air." The point is to get the students to see that nearly all the imagery, language, and structures of this text not only are familiar, but are adopted from some of the most authoritative and traditional sources in Western culture. It is, then, little wonder that beyond any analytic brilliance, Marx should appeal emotionally to his readers, inviting a transference of love to follow the translated discourses of the church, of Adam Smith, of high literature, asking them to make a faith of Marxism. But rather than seeing that power as a function of Marx's coherent vision, students should see it as an effect of paradox, the dependence of revolutionary claims on traditional values.

The final essay asks for an analysis of the text that takes account of its rhetorical invocation of authority without forgetting the insights it does provide into social relations. The students might see, for example, that as a visionary, Marx offers little more than a secular version of a Christian community, but one that no Christian society (or any other for that matter) has realized. As an analyst and critic, he never steps beyond the limits of a capitalist terminology, employing standards of values and individual freedom that the bourgeoisie would find quite familiar.[7] The students might also notice that Marx mixes economic and spiritual values with nearly as great an un-selfconsciousness as any capitalist entrepreneur. These affinities that Marx shows with the "letter" of the society he attacks opens a space for critical interpretation that goes beyond any exposition of the argument. To ask why Marx clings to traditional liberal values in the middle of a revolutionary text provides a starting point for students to explore both the structure of liberal society and the unarticulated longings at the foundations of Marx's work. Here they are on relatively open ground, with opportunity to enter the dialogue between these two great ideological systems. Once free of the obligation to love Marx or hate him—that is, to ignore, for the moment, the authority of both capitalism and Marxism—students can read him, and they can write.

When asked to write about texts, our students frequently find themselves between the wall of authority, of a *doxa* that leaves them with nothing to say, and the seas of indeterminacy where "everything is subjective." Both positions exclude them from meaningful encounters with other texts through their own writing. What I attempt through the tactics I describe here is a way of working through the pertinent paths of meaning toward something impertinent, toward a translation to set beside more or less monumental (hence immutable) authors. By choosing to discuss two writers with whom today's students are not likely to find themselves agreeing, I hope to allow students to practice the tactic without encountering the much stronger resistances that would be generated by an analysis of some beloved figure. Once Marx is made to mean something to them, then they can begin the process of questioning the language that will disclose the excesses in the text. And as long as there is an excess, there is room for interpretation and writing.

With writers or ideas that we feel committed to, that we love, this process of interpretation is more trying. Such authorities define for us what is real and true, and to reject the consoling security of the Subject Supposed to Know risks the very categories of reality and truth. This risk ultimately is not a bad one to take: the possibility of choice depends on the insecurity of having alternatives. The position I am asking my students to take is not, after all, that of a cool detachment, the conventional critical pose. Rather, I am arguing that the most significant responses come through a passionate relation to some text. Within this relation, reading against authority makes us aware of how we have come to invest our hopes and desires in the writers, politicians, and institutions—and our teachers—that create our world. But to be aware of this createdness does not mean the "creators" are to be left behind. The parents we "betray," by seeing them as human, can no longer provide us with God-like authority, but they can provide a community and a history within which it is possible to speak *with* authority—both *to* and *in the voice of* authority—without needing the certainty of absolutes.

Notes

1. The argument Thomas Kuhn makes throughout *The Structure of Scientific Revolution* displays the ways in which the desire to have a solvable puzzle prevents scientists from making, or even accepting, revolutionary scientific advances. Revolution always requires a refusal of authority.

2. I have generalized from several texts by Lacan here, but the central discussion of the Subject Supposed to Know appears in *Four Fundamental Concepts of Psychoanalysis,* chapter 18, especially 231–32.

3. Juliet Mitchell recounts the troubling moment of the child's becoming a gendered subject this way: "The castration complex ends the boy's Oedipus complex (his love for his mother) and inaugurates for the girl the one that is specifically hers: she will transfer her object love to her father who seems to have the phallus and identify with her mother who, to the girl's fury, has not. Henceforth the girl will desire to have the phallus and the boy will struggle to represent it. For this reason, for both sexes, this is the insoluble desire of their lives" (7). My point here is that masculinity implies a sort of male impersonation, a pretending to have authority that never actually exists. Rather than admit this delusion in the face of the increasing

power women are gaining in the world, the patriarchal structure has invited women to join the impersonation, retaining the form of phallic authority, no matter which sex embodies it.

4. Much of what has come to be known as "deconstruction" is closely related to such a violation of the "integrity" of the text. See, for an early example, Derrida's discussion of the "supplement" in *Of Grammatology* (144–45).

5. Roland Barthes discusses the relation of *doxa* to paradox in an essay on teaching. He writes: "A new discourse can only emerge as the *paradox* which goes against (and often goes for) the surrounding or preceding *doxa,* can only see the day as difference, distinction, working loose *against* what sticks to it" (200). To speak with a new voice, consequently, does not imply the ignoring of meaning, but a working within meaning, though without closure. I am suggesting a teaching of writing that would lead to a similarly nonconclusive dialectic of writing and reading.

6. Samuel Beer's introduction to the Crofts Classics edition and A. J. P. Taylor's to the Penguin provide good examples of this editorial discretion.

7. Jean Baudrillard presents a very useful discussion of the ways in which Marx's language is bound up in that of capitalism in *The Mirror of Production.*

Works Cited

Barthes, Roland. "Writers, Intellectuals, Teachers." *Image–Music–Text.* Trans. Stephen Heath. New York: Hill, 1977. 190–215.

Baudrillard, Jean. *The Mirror of Production.* Trans. Mark Poster. St. Louis: Telos, 1975.

Beer, Samuel H. Introduction. *The Communist Manifesto.* By Karl Marx and Friedrich Engels. Crofts Classics. Arlington Heights, IL.: AHM, 1955. vii–xxix.

Derrida, Jacques. *Of Grammatology.* Trans. Gayatri Chakravorty Spivak. Baltimore: Johns Hopkins UP, 1976.

Felman, Shoshana. "Psychoanalysis and Education: Teaching Terminable and Interminable." *Yale French Studies* 63 (1982): 21–44.

Gallop, Jane. *Reading Lacan.* Ithaca, NY: Cornell UP, 1985.

Kuhn, Thomas S. *The Structure of Scientific Revolution,* 2nd ed. Chicago: U of Chicago P, 1970.

Lacan, Jacques. *Four Fundamentals of Psychoanalysis*. Trans. Alan Sheridan. New York: Norton, 1978.

Mitchell, Juliet. Introduction—I. *Feminine Sexuality*. By Jacques Lacan and the *école freudienne*. Ed. Juliet Mitchell and Jacqueline Rose. Trans. Jacqueline Rose. New York: Norton, 1982. 1–26.

Morgan, Marabel. *The Total Woman*. New York: Simon, Pocket, 1973.

Taylor, A. J. P. Introduction. *The Communist Manifesto*. London: Penguin, 1967. 7–47.

4

Freud and the Teaching
of Interpretation

*Patricia Donahue and
Ellen Quandahl*

The theory that reading is composing—an open-ended, investigative and active process—is hardly new. Over the past few years, writing teachers have turned their attention to reading and extended the useful term *process* to describe not only the recursive movement among the pre-writing, drafting, and revising stages of writing, but also the construction of meaning through reading. The theories they have drawn on range from the work of reading researchers like Harry Singer, Frank Smith, and Cooper and Petrosky, to critical theorists like Wolfgang Iser, Louise Rosenblatt, and Roland Barthes. While it is difficult to generalize about such wide-ranging work, a quick review of the literature of "constructive" reading shows agreement on one point: the power of conventions, or schemata, to shape our understanding of a text. But the language for naming this phenomenon is divergent. Reading researchers describe the process of composing meaning in apparently neutral terms—comprehending, reading for meaning, learning from text—and some separate a literal from an interpretive level of reading, using Benjamin Bloom's taxonomy (89–90), influential since the 1950s.[1] Critical theorists, on the other hand, show that all composed meanings are interpretations; this is the view we want to illustrate as we describe, theoretically and practically, a sequence of writing assignments we used to encourage interpretation in our introductory composition classes.

In our view, the same questions asked by critical theory—what is reading, what is the status of a text, how do we clarify approaches to interpretation—are questions to be asked by composition teachers, whose job is to teach students how to compose readings of texts, literary and nonliterary, written and nonwritten. With this aim in mind, we agreed to define interpretation as a process of both reading *and* writing. We discarded conventional injunctions to "look at the words," as if simply gazing at words on the page would force them into meaning. We insisted instead that good readers must understand the assumptions that determine what they see, that good writers do not wait for meaning to take shape, and that a text itself imposes constraints upon the kinds of reading we can produce. We thought that Freud's famous study *Dora: An Analysis of a Case of Hysteria* would be exemplary for this kind of approach, and we used it both as a model of the interpretive process and as the subject of our reading and writing assignments.

Freud's case studies are customarily used by literary critics to provide a heuristic for identifying latent meanings and the hidden structure of textual dream work. But we found the case study of Dora useful for making explicit some ways of using and observing conventions to read a text, a process that conflates reading and writing. Freud reads his clients' stories by rewriting them. Using psychoanalysis as a schema, or master narrative, he reorganizes their details into a new story (one that also illustrates the themes of the psychoanalytic story). He compares himself to a fiction-writer, who ascribes to Dora "a fine poetic conflict" (77). His task as psycho-analyst is clearly to rewrite or translate events by placing them in the context of a larger narrative, and to make explicit the connections that seem to be hidden: "I suspect that we are here concerned with unconscious processes of thought which are twined around a pre-existing structure of organic connections, such as festoons of flowers are twined around a wire; . . . [A] knowledge of the thought-connec-tions . . . is of a value which cannot be exaggerated for clearing up the symptoms" (104).

Following Freud, we began with the assumption that interpreta-tion is a translation or a transformation of a text rather than a substitution of one kind of text for another. When he interprets Dora's dreams, Freud translates the dream images into another syntax, so that the images are available in a new way: "I learnt how to translate the language of dreams into the forms of expression of our own thought-language, which can be understood without further help" (29). We taught our students that they in turn were transforming Freud's text when they used details from it in their own sentences, for then they recontextualized them, establishing an alternative set of connections. They were interpreting even when they summarized or paraphrased. We explained that their summaries "reworked" a text by responding to its obvious repetitions or what it seemed intentionally to stress. Summary is an interpretive act because it misreads an original, using the convention of examining only primary, dominant possibilities.

From our first assumption, three strategic definitions followed. First (and in this we are also following Freud), to interpret is to connect ideas, to create relationships among them. These relationships can be, for example, chronological, repetitive, and causal. To begin to interpret Freud's texts, therefore, students first had to identify his efforts to establish a narrative or to create similarities and differences. Freud comments that patients often cannot give an ordered history of their lives and break connections when they alter the chronology of events: "The connections—even the ostensible ones—are for the most part incoherent, and the sequence of different events is uncertain. . . . It is only towards the end of the treatment that we have before us an intelligible, consistent, and unbroken case history" (31–32). One of the aims of his analysis is therefore to restore connections to the patient's conscious mind. As a reader of Dora's story, Freud looks for verbal clues that signal relationships. He says, for example, "It is a rule of psychoanalytic technique that an internal connection which is still undisclosed will announce its presence by means of a contiguity . . . of associations" (55). And later: "We have already learnt that a single symptom corresponds quite regularly to several meanings *simultaneously*. We may now add that it can express several meanings in *succession*" (70). In turn, there are verbal clues to reading Freud's study. They consist of words as simple as *and* and *but,* or as complicated as the reversals and oppositions Freud uses as he revises an earlier idea in light of new information. While students can hunt for these connectors and then understand the intended relationships between things, they can also, we told them, rewrite the text and impose upon it another chain of connections. They can trace within it patterns that Freud may not be aware of, if we give them a new schema to work with. To interpret, then, is to transform a text by selecting and reordering elements of it in new connections of one's own making.

From this follows our second strategic definition. To interpret requires readers to identify both a text's insights and its blindnesses (to use the words of Kenneth Burke and Paul de Man). Freud reads Dora in just this way: "She might be blind in one direction, but she was sharp-sighted in the other" (52). To read interpretively, students needed to learn that texts, like analysands, articulate some statements more strongly than others. They produce significant repetitions, material that seems to be at the center and to reveal intention: "Dora's incessant repetitions of the same thought . . . made it possible to derive still further important material from the analysis" (71). Students therefore need to train their sight to perceive the conceptual center of a textual system as well as its margins. Not to do so would mean that they would always allow another's language to dominate their own sensibilities. They would, in other words, be mastered, and we wanted them, on the contrary, to resist a text's dominant meanings, to read "otherwise." Thus we wanted them not merely to dismiss Freud, when he seemed too complicated or too outrageous, but to notice, for example, that when Freud repeatedly defends Herr K. (Dora's suitor, the husband of her father's mistress), apparently identifying with him, Freud dismisses Dora herself. His insight by identification into Herr K. made him in some ways blind to his client and unaware of the entire tangle of motives. (For this reason, many feminists have discussed "hysteria" as a signifier that displaces feminine desire into a masculine psychology.) Freud's assumptions and practices suggest a point of view, a way of privileging ideas and making them persuasive. Freud reveals his persuasive intent with phrases like "The patients themselves are easy to convince" (66), and "Dora disputed the fact [of Freud's interpretation] no longer" (125). Such attempts to exert power are observable in all texts. By reading Freud, students can learn that interpretations assert authority by naturalizing certain arguments (making them appear acceptable and true) and marginalizing others (labeling them unacceptable, inappropriate, or bogus).

Finally, we defined interpretation as a process of both identification and resistance. One of our most common complaints about students' assessment of texts is that they tend to record in them only the most banal, the most trivial of ideas. Students leap to identify in a difficult work something they know; they project themselves into the language and engage in what Iser calls "consistency-building" (118–29). While that is not a bad starting point, especially if they come to recognize the conceptual baggage they carry with them as readers, it is a poor ending. We hoped to bring students to a point where they could both identify within a text some commonsensical assumptions and then move beyond them to see how, through the act of reading, complicated works frequently resist simpleminded conclusions. We hoped they could begin to recognize ideas as personal and social compositions and to realize that culture often speaks through the scrim of a text.

Having established our working definitions, we then translated them into the classroom idiom. Through three assignments, our students explored different ways of constructing meanings, of reading a text. We had them read Freud, not to learn about the origins of psychoanalysis or the emotions of the nineteenth-century teenager, but to read a text by organizing it in different ways: chronologically, analytically, and dramatically.

We should mention that our students had been labeled special action or affirmative action, and placed in an intensive version of UCLA's freshman writing sequence in the course prerequisite to the one all freshmen must pass. They were black, Hispanic, and Filipino, mostly local, but not from the best high schools. Their placement in the program reinforced what they knew all too well—that they had a good chance of failing. We offer this profile not to introduce a particular success story, but to show the possibility of a dignified, university-level curriculum, one with strong theoretical underpinnings, for poorly prepared students. In many so-called remedial programs around the country, students like these are still being given workbook drills in grammar, spelling, and sentence-combining. In more enlightened programs, the common wisdom about such students is that they be given material that makes them feel immediately confident and powerful, that one not teach over their heads. Frequently they are given relatively easy reading, or short, unrelated essays, perhaps representative of university discourse, but dissociated from an interpretive context. But rather than preparing them for the sustained analytical inquiry we most want them to master, the leap from one amputated text to another models disjunction and loose coordination, patterns with which they are all too familiar.

In response to this problem, we designed a sequence of writing assignments moving among several kinds of interpretation, and each requiring that the students had read the entire case history of Dora. The case history, as we know, concerns an eighteen-year-old woman, Dora, who is brought to Freud by her father, against her will, for psychoanalytical treatment of her psychosomatic symptoms and "hysteria." Freud alternates between offering his readers details that Dora reveals about herself and interpreting those details as he moves backward and forward in time, detective like, among the incidents he has collected.

Our students, during the first discussion in both of our classes, said that they couldn't read the case, it was too hard, they couldn't make anything of it. When pressed, they said they could understand a few things, the parts about Dora: she had a cough, a man kissed her in his office one day, something happened by a lake. They could make nothing of the case beyond those incidents in the life of a young woman. So it was to these details we directed their attention for the first assignment. We asked them to rewrite Dora's story in chronological order. This involved searching the whole text for details given in an order moving repeatedly from present to past, and attempting to distill the sequence of events from Freud's comments about them. We began with this task because we wanted to work with, rather than against, our students' interests, not because we thought the creation of narrative a simple task to be done before more difficult ones. As Shirley Brice Heath points out, growth in literacy "does not require a tight, linear order of instruction that breaks down small sets and subsets of skills into isolated, sequential hierarchies" (24). We wanted the students to find their own point of entry into the text, and they were clearly interested in the details of Dora's life. We also wanted to involve them immediately with the whole text and to suggest that they could use the text, rather than be overwhelmed by it: they could move from confusion to control.

Discussing these first papers in class, the students noticed that Freud did not really tell the beginning of the story until the end, and that this is something a writer might do, maintaining suspense to keep a reader interested. They also began to see that it was extremely difficult to separate Dora's story from what Freud makes of it, since he, after all, is the teller. By imagining the fullness of Dora's life and realizing that Freud's reading is incomplete (he leaves out much of her experience to focus upon the traumatic events), they could see that the assumptions they had about "the story of a life" limited their reading. They had to learn that Dora's history is Freud's interpretation, his story, if they were to construct for the text other possibilities.

The second assignment therefore directed the students to Freud's interpretations, his efforts to emphasize and deemphasize certain elements of Dora's reconstructed experience. We asked the students to paraphrase three small pieces of the intepretation, after we had done one paraphrase together in class. We looked at the words and patterns Freud tended most to repeat, for paraphrase reproduces a text's emphases. We asked the students to collect and group the repetitions from their own paraphrases. Then, in the paper, they were to characterize Freud's method of analysis, his technique as an analytic investigator, by describing the connections he typically makes. These connections were of various kinds: *chronological* (connections that created a narrative), *repetitive* (connections that established similarities among symptoms), *causal* (Freud's efforts to explain symptoms in terms of prior experiences), and *psychological* (connections between the individual utterance and psychoanalytic vocabulary).

This paper was the most difficult, requiring synthesis of the connections we had been studying together. But in writing it, students saw that to interpret is to look from a point of view, a set of assumptions, Freud's as well as their own. They found that Freud worked like a detective, collecting clues, connecting them, and excluding from his reading details that did not fit. His reading was not arbitrary, but revealed his ideas about disease and cure, about the structure of all "good" psychoanalytical stories, about the behavior acceptable to eighteen-year-old women. In writing about Freud, the students came to read like him, engaging in the process of decision-making that is central to all interpretation. They had to decide what to include and what to exclude in their "rewriting" of Freud, and they noticed that their assumptions about reading influenced what they wrote. It became clear to them that no reading, and for that matter no act of writing, is comprehensive, identical with the original.

The final assignment in the sequence asked the students to describe a session with Freud, a conversation between Freud and Dora, from Dora's point of view. They were to incorporate an event from her life, which they knew very well from the first assignment, and describe how Freud analyzed it, which they knew very well from the second assignment, but this time with Dora as the teller. They were to attempt to restore Dora's voice and allow her to comment on Freud's judgments.

This reading required the students to create for the text still another pattern of meaning as they examined Dora's significant silences and looked closely at Freud's use of her words. It also required them to consider Freud's point of view as a product of his training as a psychoanalyst, his experience as a nineteenth-century male, husband, and father, and his commitment to certain perspectives. For example, Freud's "aesthetics of distaste" leads him to criticize Dora's unwillingness to accept the attentions of a man "still quite young and of prepossessing appearance" (44), whose proposals were neither "tactless nor offensive" (54). Our students had to situate Freud's text, in other words, in the contexts of history, gender, and discipline, and see it as a construct that is cultural as well as personal. Not surprisingly, many of their Doras were critical and angry with Freud. For example, some wrote that, as Dora, they were upset that Freud thought it unnatural to be disgusted by the kisses of an older man. Others thought that Freud was appropriating her life by not allowing her a chance to disagree with him or to disapprove of her manipulative family. Such retellings were clearly their own interpretations of Freud's analysis, although guided by the text rather than personal fancy. And, had it not been the end of the quarter, they could well have been the basis of a fourth project, in which the students translated their narrative or dramatic accounts into expository interpretations.

Because a critical pedagogy embeds theory within practice, it can be difficult to outline systematically. Let us then summarize what for us were the significant issues. Certainly one such issue is that interpretive reading requires first a writing and then a rewriting of a text. Because our students needed to begin somewhere, we encouraged them to employ familiar cultural codes—the "reference codes" Barthes speaks of (18–21)—and write the text as a mirror of ideas they could relate or "refer" to (such as the abuse of Dora by her father, Herr K, and Freud). But because we knew that without our intervention they would not have gone any further, attempted any "rewriting," we designed a second assignment that encouraged them to see the text a second time and move beyond consistency-building. To see the text differently, as a spark for their composing activity, the students had to resist their assumptions as well as the text's intentional patterns. They had to examine the repressions of both patient and analyst, and to rewrite Freud's story as he had rewritten Dora's. To put this still more directly, we could say that our students first had to learn the authorized discourses (recognize their assumptions and the text's intentions) before they could read against them. And to read "otherwise," they had to use what they had learned from Freud as a reader. Our assignments, we want to emphasize, explicitly led them through these stages: we left little to chance.

Another important issue involves our students' having been labeled as basic writers. We refer once again to this label to suggest that the theory of reading (and reciprocally of writing) examined here is brought into high relief with such students. What distinguishes basic writers, of course, is their weak understanding of the conventions of meaning, their unfamiliarity with the language of academic discourse, their lack of control over interpretive idioms. With them, our pedagogical methods had to become pointedly direct. As David Bartholomae tells us, all students (especially basic writers) "need to learn to extend themselves into the commonplaces, set phrases, rituals, gestures, habits of mind, tricks of persuasion, obligatory conclusions, and necessary connections that determine what 'might be said' and constitute knowledge within the various branches of our academic community" (11). In line with his recommendation, we attempted to initiate our basic writers into the conventions of academic discourse, illustrate for them our reading and writing practices, teach them the processes of interpretation. *Dora* provided a vehicle, enabling us to build our students' confidence in handling "hard books," the language they are expected to manage in most classes. More importantly, it enabled us to welcome them into our community of "insiders." Our experience with basic students brought attention to a general principle: all reading pedagogy needs to be illustrative. Reading is bound by rules, stipulated as well as secret, of the disciplines and culture. Freud reveals his backstage secrets to us; we can reveal ours to our students. If the reading researchers and critical theorists are right (and we are assuming they are), reading is the interpretive process of unfolding and resisting the meaning of intentional objects or events. And it is a process that must (and can) be taught. The traditional faith in reading as a "natural," obvious, and commonsensical activity ignores the reality of process and pedagogy.

In discussing what our students learned, we have, of course, appropriated and translated their language. To keep our focus on how we used theory in the classroom, we have chosen not to cite their essays; that would be the subject of another essay, another case study. But for readers who wonder whether these assignments "worked," we can offer these claims: On the final examination (which was universitywide, not specific to our classes, and which asked students to write about a text distributed before the exam), our students performed better than had students in our previous classes. (Perhaps we had exceptional students.) During the second quarter, when we taught another case study (*The Wolf Man*), students came by the office and said things like, "In the fall we couldn't read this stuff. Now we can." They no longer felt defeated when assigned difficult academic material, but instead knew they could approach the texts confidently. They owned some powerful tools. Most important among these subjective claims, we sensed that our students engaged the material and were willing to write about it. This quality of engagement in their writing convinced us that they had improved. They could now talk about texts.

Finally, our work with Freud provided us, as instructors, with a model for pedagogy. We learned that we can turn to theory for ways of doing as well as seeing. As we have repeatedly mentioned, our theory of the interpretive process was derived from and influenced by Freud's performance as a reader. Within his text, he translates and transforms, identifies significant verbal clusters, establishes the dominance of some interpretive possibilities over others, and presents his own writing as a reading of another's constructs and experiences. By following Freud's therapeutic model, we helped our students to compose and decompose assumptions about what they thought they knew, while at the same time providing them with an alternative model of reading, another process, another story. And by using Freud as an example of one reader reading, we entered the larger conversation now so active within several disciplines, that of the process of interpretation and the composing of meaning.

Notes

1. For example, Falke 127; Flynn 146.

Works Cited

Barthes, Roland. *S/Z*. New York: Hill, 1974.

Bartholomae, David. "Inventing the University." *Journal of Basic Writing* 5.1 (1986): 4–23.

Bloom, Benjamin S., ed. *Taxonomy of Educational Objectives*. New York: McKay, 1956.

Burke, Kenneth. *Attitudes Toward History*. Berkeley: U of California P, 1984.

Cooper, Charles R., and Anthony R. Petrosky. "A Psycho-Linguistic View of the Fluent Reading Process." *Journal of Reading* (1976): 184–201.

De Man, Paul. *Blindness and Insight*. Minneapolis: U of Minnesota P, 1983.

Falke, Anne. "What Every Educator Should Know about Reading Research." *Language Connections*. Ed. Toby Fulwiler and Art Young. Urbana: NCTE, 1982. 123–37.

Flynn, Elizabeth. "Reconciling Readers and Texts." *Language Connections*. 139–52.

Freud, Sigmund. *Dora: An Analysis of a Case of Hysteria*. Ed. Philip Rieff. New York: Collier, 1963.

Gibson, Eleanor J., and Harry Levin. *The Psychology of Reading*. Cambridge: MIT, 1976.

Heath, Shirley Brice. "The Functions and Uses of Literacy." *Literacy, Society, and Schooling*. Ed. Suzanne de Castell, Allan Luke, and Kiernan Egan. Cambridge: Cambridge UP, 1986. 15–26.

Iser, Wolfgang. *The Act of Reading*. Baltimore: Johns Hopkins UP, 1978.

Rosenblatt, Louise. *The Reader, the Text, the Poem: The Transactional Theory of the Literary Work*. Carbondale: Southern Illinois UP, 1978.

Singer, Harry. "A Century of Landmarks in Reading and Learning from Text at the High School Level: Research, Theories, and Instructional Strategies." *Journal of Reading* (1983): 332–42.

Smith, Frank. *Understanding Reading: A Psycholinguistic Analysis of Reading and Learning to Read*. New York: Holt, 1971.

5

Conversations with the Social Text

Nina Schwartz

Roland Barthes identifies the origin of the essays collected in *Mythologies* as "a feeling of impatience at the sight of the 'naturalness' with which newspapers, art and common sense constantly dress up a reality which, even though it is the one we live in, is undoubtedly determined by history. . . . I resented seeing Nature and History confused at every turn, and I wanted to track down, in the decorative display of *what-goes-without-saying,* the ideological abuse which, in my view, is hidden there" (*Mythologies* 11). By "ideological abuse," Barthes refers to a culture's representation of itself in the media and elsewhere as an unproblematic "translation" of natural law into social practices and institutions. The subjects of Barthes' essays, then, are both the materials and the mechanisms through which the confusion of nature and culture occurs in his society. Although he takes his examples from French bourgeois culture of the 1950s, his pieces sufficiently illuminate contemporary American social phenomena to guide first-year students asked to carry on a similar kind of cultural analysis.

Such analytic work is suited to writing classes because it provides a reason to consider language in all its complexity. But Barthes' pertinence to the writing course derives from something else as well, the fact that a text like *Mythologies* explicitly addresses one of the writing teacher's greatest frustrations: students' difficulty in "finding something to say." Sometimes they cannot think of anything to say because they have not been taught analytic discourse yet; but at the same time, they are often resistant to learning that discourse because they cannot figure out what its purpose might be outside of the composition class. For the most part, that is, the world seems to many students to be a closed and nonproblematic system in which things are what they are for good reasons. The "good reasons," however, are by nature difficult to identify or define, because they are the stuff of "commonsense," precisely one of those social orders that passes for essential or absolute. Because students assume that they, and we, "already know" the answers to questions about their beliefs, they find it difficult to make a case to support them, or even to say clearly what those beliefs are. Students, that is, failing to distinguish between the natural and the social, the inevitable and the conventional, cannot help but develop a world view that keeps them relatively inarticulate. And their silence persists despite our claims that it is often in what-goes-without-saying that interesting thought, conversation, and writing lie.

We all "know," for example, why some people have more money than others: they earned it or they inherited it—either way, it belongs to them, and people who question the rights of the rich frequently have an ax to grind, are not objective, that is, do not have much money themselves. Similarly, everyone knows why students want to join fraternities or sororities: because that is where one finds a social life and friends, dates and business contacts. These reasons are obvious to anyone who lives inside the university culture and knows the codes, so students think that articulating them is beside the point. And to some degree, of course, they are right, since the examples I have mentioned above depend on assumptions that do not, for the initiated, require explanation. But what students need to understand is that our putative reasons for doing or thinking things are not always simple. To the extent that reasons go without saying, they can themselves be read as symptoms of something else, something more complicated, less flattering, and worst of all, less "logical" than they seem to be. They can be alibis, that is, for something that they and we work hard to disguise from ourselves.

The apparently sensible nature of the world not only keeps students quiet; it leads to a potentially dangerous understanding of the individual's relation to this world. Reading or understanding comes to seem a passive and uncomplicated *reception* of the truth, facts, or reality that some authoritative figure has discovered; writing or explaining is merely the straightforward reproduction of the preexisting truth that has been uncomplicatedly received. Students, that is, can hardly be expected to exemplify in their own writing a sophisticated understanding of why they think one thing rather than another until they have learned to see their views as something other than inevitable. And they can hardly be expected to subject their interpretive habits to self-conscious analysis until they have learned more about the ways in which other writers and thinkers arrive at and reveal their interpretive habits and assumptions. The orderly and circular relation of reading to writing, of students to the world in which they live, needs to be disturbed, then, because it is from the nonappearance of problems, confusion, and contradiction that silence and complacency derive. Many of us who work in composition have come to see the writing class as a good place—perhaps even the best—to initiate a systematic and focused disruption of normative meanings, of commonsensical understandings.

In an essay called "Composition and Decomposition," J. Hillis Miller offers a now fairly commonplace definition of writing and reading as two related forms of rhetoric: writing, he says, is "rhetoric as persuasion. It works by synthesis. Reading, on the other hand, is decomposition, . . . the analysis or untying of the links that bind a piece of language together so that the reader can see how it works and make sure he has grasped its meaning correctly" (42). In marking out this difference, Miller implicitly identifies one problem that many writing teachers have confronted: that attention to reading often conflicts with or even impedes the teaching of more explicitly "practical" writing skills. For one thing, composition teachers are often accused of trying to turn the writing class into a literature class, of preferring to teach reading rather than writing because it allows us to talk about what is supposed to be our "real" love, great literature. But a more serious, because more apparently demonstrable charge has been leveled at attempts to integrate reading and writing: despite our theoretical claims that the two are inextricably bound and even simultaneous interpretive processes, they do not always appear to be so. The problem is that reading does not always make things clear. When it works properly, critically, or "literarily," reading has the potential to "confuse" things by introducing too many possibilities for meaning. Because we can focus on so many elements of a text's production of meaning—diction and tone, allusion and metaphor, persona and argument, example and logic—and on the potential conflicts among these elements, we may find ourselves introducing a whole range of possibilities for interesting but multivalent or disunified discussion. In the process, we threaten to violate precisely those principles of selection that we teach students to employ in distinguishing between the pertinent and the impertinent, the central and the tangential, in their own writing. Problems arise, that is, when we direct our students to read complicatedly but to write clearly. Clarity and those other privileged features of academic prose—unity, directness, sincerity—may seem inconsistent with the "surplus" of meanings that reading discloses. How can we invite students to see so much but to say so little? How can we exclude the effects of their reading from the essays they write for us? How can we encourage them to explore the margins of the texts they read but insist that they preserve the virtues of unity and centrality in their own texts?

Miller claims that "no skillful composition is possible without that prior act of decomposition practiced through reading models of composition by others" (42); but this is a fact that our pedagogy belies when we force students to exclude the products of their "decomposing" activities from their compositions, to learn to *control* their essays. Our pedagogical conflicts, however, reproduce a conflict inherent in the culture itself, a contradiction or discontinuity within the model of individuality that the culture propagates. We believe in the value and the possibility of "self-control," of the "ego" as policelike mediator between social requirements and personal desires, despite the fact that such "control" is frequently achieved only by ignoring or failing to see what cannot be controlled. In our complicated world, the ideal of self-control is a delusion to which we remain committed even in the face of its practical limits. But perhaps our own teaching dilemma can communicate something of this larger problem to students.

The metaphor of "conversation" is helpful here in articulating the relation between reading and writing that we might put in place of the model of reception our teaching practices sometimes encourage. The term is defined as "an act or instance of talking together, of exchanging ideas or opinions." The mere idea of "exchange" is an important one for our students to understand, because it implies a giving up of one thing for a substitute or alternative. Of course, what is "given up" in such an exchange is not necessarily a particular opinion, to be substituted by someone else's. What I "give up" in conversation is rather a particular kind of closure or certainty: no exchange occurs without some risk, however minimal, to my ideas and opinions. And the substitute I receive in exchange for the old certainty is a new role, one constituted by a responsibility to another. In this role, that is, I take on the responsibility for my own views, for thinking reflectively about what they are and why I hold them. And I take on as well the responsibility for interpreting and understanding the views of the other. I must recognize, that is, that I have a world view and that not everyone shares it; that I am like others, in short, not necessarily because we all think alike but because my view, like any other, makes "good sense" only within a particular and limited context.

This exchange, then, is not necessarily an easy one, however much its difficulties are belied by the dictionary definition of the term. "Conversation" may name the act of talking together informally, but the word itself comes from a root that complicates such a meaning. The intransitive verb *to converse* has as its root meaning "to live with, to keep company with, to turn around." This etymology suggests the complexities of "conversation" when it is considered seriously: to live with other people is a difficult enterprise precisely because it requires a willingness to keep "turning" ourselves around, sometimes inside out, sometimes into something we normally are not, in order to accommodate the needs of being together. The fact that we perform these turns in and through language makes them even more complex than they might otherwise seem to be. In the face of such difficulties, we may be strongly tempted to substitute a vocal silence, a nonconversation based on supposedly shared assumptions. That is, a myth of agreement stands in for real conversation, although it may go without saying.

Barthes' discussion of "myth" provides a model for the dynamic and even aggressively disruptive relation of reading and writing that I have described through the word *conversation*. As Barthes defines the term, myth is first of all a mode of representation that works to produce a confusion between nature and culture. In effect, myth is responsible for transforming social conventions into "second nature," our commonsense ways of acting in and thinking about the world. It is thus one of the forces that keep us quiet in the face of questions about our beliefs. In being required to discover and analyze some of the social texts—fashion, toys, film, advertising, or conventional writing—that make up the realities in which we live, students are also encouraged to recognize and articulate the implicit values and beliefs that inform their understanding of the world and motivate their behavior in it. Students can make this discovery first by reading selections from *Mythologies* to familiarize themselves with some of Barthes' basic assumptions about social sign systems. Writing summaries, paraphrases, and then analyses of his arguments, students reinforce their understanding of his method. As they become more adept at reading, they can also take on more complicated analyses of social myths that Barthes does not discuss. They can imitate his method, that is, by reading and writing about other problems of understanding that they encounter in their own lives and studies, without necessarily reproducing the same conclusions he reaches.

But the step from analyzing Barthes' texts to imitating his method is not an easy one. As any reader of Barthes knows, his work is dense, elliptical, and sometimes seemingly impenetrable. One must work carefully, in an actively "interventionist" way, to translate very abstract claims into concretely analyzable examples and so test his assertions against the real world. But the difficulty of reading Barthes actually begins to prepare students to carry on a work like his outside of his texts. The very density of his prose, that is, may seem to students a "mistake" similar to one they are often accused of making, the mistake of assuming a reader's immediate under-standing of his meaning. But as they work to interpret Barthes' compressed terms and "thick language" (*Image–Music–Text* 168), they achieve firsthand experience of the kind of translation that needs to take place in any real reading activity, no matter how apparently transparent a text may seem. They have to make the text's implicit logic explicit, first to themselves and then to another reader. The complexity of Barthes' writing is an extreme example of the actual complexity of all language, a quality that is easy to over-look or repress because of the familiar contexts that normally make us sure we know what someone means, whether he or she says it "clearly" or not.

As they practice this activity in informal paraphrases of particu-larly troublesome passages, students become more adept and eventu-ally less antagonistic toward the texts they are reading. And they also begin to recognize a pattern in Barthes' work: he never says explicitly in *Mythologies* what the "myth" is in the cultural situation he describes. Instead, he exposes in that situation a gap or internal contradiction that readers must interpret in order to establish a "new" coherence to replace the old one that has been disrupted. The gap, then, provides entrance into the myth, but it does not perform that undisguising activity for us—we have to do that ourselves. We cannot simply receive the "truth" of Barthes' *Mythologies,* because there is not one, at least not one that exists without readers' partici-pation. The apparent failure to be clear then, may actually be an intentional refusal-to-say, one that demands an active effort from the reader to "complete" the text's meaning.

In his analysis of French toys ("Toys"), for example, clearly trans-
ferable to American toys, Barthes notes that "one could not find a
better illustration of the fact that the adult . . . sees the child as
another self. All the toys one commonly sees are essentially a micro-
cosm of the adult world; they are all reduced copies of human objects,
as if in the eyes of the public the child was, all told, nothing but a
smaller man, a homunculus to whom must be supplied objects of his
own size" (*Mythologies* 53). Students tend to interpret these claims
at first in reasonable but not particularly challenging ways: Barthes
must mean that toys make children grow up too fast or that they
restrict children's imaginative freedom. An analysis of the toys we
produce for children, they see, reveals the extent to which our culture
identifies childhood specifically as *training,* not just for adulthood,
but for specific predetermined roles.

Such arguments generally seem familiar to students, and in the
formal summaries they write of this essay, I encourage them to say
what they know, to associate freely between what Barthes writes
and what they remember from other analyses of American toys. But
they do this in part so they can eventually see what is different about
Barthes' argument. Students may recall, for example, the feminist
argument that giving little girls baby dolls and tea sets, ironing
boards and fashion models encourages sexual stereotypes and a lack
of imagination about future roles and professions. Similarly, they
know that parents and educators express concern over the violence
and aggression that toy guns and other weapons encourage in all
children, but particularly in little boys. Barthes would no doubt
agree with these assessments of the hidden agendas implicit in the
toys we give our children. But he is defining a different and even
more pervasive effect of toys, one that is hard to figure out at first.
In the summaries students have written, we now pay particular
attention to those elements of Barthes' analysis of toys that have
been "left out"—because they seemed either unimportant, unfamiliar, or uninterpretable. We make the next phase of our discussion,
that is, what students could not include in their own "reproduction"
of Barthes without simply repeating his language, what they could
not translate into their own terms. In the essay on toys, the difficulty
usually comes down to a single claim: within this world of miniatur-
ized but faithful copies of adult objects, Barthes says, "the child can
only identify himself as owner, as user, never as creator; he does not
invent the world, he uses it: there are prepared for him, actions
without adventure, without wonder, without joy" (*Mythologies* 54).

Barthes does not discuss in any detail either what he means by this claim or the consequences of such training of children, and here students' most difficult task begins (though it does not end). They must try to imagine and articulate exactly what it means to be "[an] owner, [a] user, never [a] creator." That difficulty, in fact, becomes the center of the formal paper students write for this unit of the course: an analysis of what Barthes means when he says that "ownership" is the source of an identity in our culture. But this claim is one students do not always register as significant, or at least not in its entirety. Students "see" and understand the second and third clauses describing what toys teach a child—"he does not invent the world, he uses it: there are prepared for him, actions without adventure, without wonder, without joy"—because these claims seem to be about a value they have been taught is important: individual freedom. But the first clause, about ownership, is hard for them to interpret.

Both the difficulty and the value of this effort, however, derive from the same source: students are being asked to think critically about their own culturally formed assumptions from inside the language that inculcates and perpetuates those assumptions. For most Americans, that is, the title *owner* is one to be attained, not questioned: the culture we live in has worked hard and successfully to make such questioning seem not just unnecessary but crazy. After all, ownership is supposed to be the way "internal" qualities like intelligence, perseverance, willpower, and determination manifest themselves externally. Things, like money, are merely the secondary signifiers of essential characteristics that really are worthy of our respect and admiration. Nevertheless, provoked by Barthes' "confusing" assertion, students can be pushed to consider both the meaning and the significance of ownership and its alternatives, if indeed there are any. Ownership, they can begin to formulate, institutes a hierarchy—the owner over the owned, as well as over those who do not own—and in the process confers a kind of "mastery" or authority on the owner. By virtue of his or her possession of something, the owner achieves a sense of significance.

The study questions accompanying the formal assignment ask students to consider a number of issues. One question is why, for example, we frequently seek to own much more than is necessary for either comfort or convenience. In their written responses, students comment, often very articulately, on the "psychological" function of possessing many things, the way it communicates to others, like friends and family, the extent of our success or the range of our interests. Asked about the personal consequences of this method for achieving an identity, some writers joke that it is merely expensive, but others can begin to recognize the intriguing paradox: that "ownership" costs, more than money, a certain "independence" that we as Americans like to imagine we possess. If my sense of importance derives from what I own, for example, then I become curiously and somehow inappropriately dependent on the thing I am supposed to be master of to signify to myself and others that I am indeed a master. One of the final study questions asks what in our culture would be lost if there were another way for the majority of citizens to identify themselves: if the assignment and our classroom discussions have been effective, students have started to see that our entire economic system depends to a great extent on the kind of subjectivity instituted by the models of ownership and consumption promulgated in toys.

The "training" begun by toys, then, defines the "natural" condition of humanness as possession, *consumption*. The child is thereby prepared to enter the bourgeois world complete with the typical and necessary adult desire *to possess* all the things that will mark him or her as a successful member of the world that already exists, and all the authority that attends the identity of *owner* in our culture. Based on Barthes' analysis, students can begin to see how the toys we think of as innately pleasurable function in fact to prepare a particular economic myth: that owning is itself a pleasure, perhaps the supreme or only pleasure that children should look forward to enjoying. One effect of such an early education to this myth is to stabilize a certain economic and social order. In producing children as consumers, we ensure the continued existence of a market for the goods our industries manufacture, and we ensure as well that few children will try to identify themselves in ways that might threaten the status quo. As Barthes explains, "the end of myths is to immobilize the world: they must suggest and mimic a universal order which has fixated once and for all the hierarchy of possessions" (*Mythologies* 155). The myth implicit in toys is that the condition of the consumer is a natural one: of course we give our children toys that imitate the forms of the adult world, because the adult world is not just the one that exists, but the one that *should* exist. The power to own really *does* indicate the owner's achievement of a desirable and important identity in the world, and those who cannot achieve such an identity are unfortunately lacking in the natural qualities that lead to success: "We reach here the very principle of myth: it transforms history into nature. . . . what causes mythical speech to be uttered is perfectly explicit, but it is immediately frozen into something natural; it is not read as a motive, but as a reason" (*Mythologies* 129).

Indeed, toys and the myth of ownership that they perpetuate suggest something more particular about the problem our students face in learning to read and write analytically, which is one very important reason for getting them to articulate that myth as fully as they can. As children are taught by their toys to believe in the naturalness of consumption as the model of adult living, so have our college students been taught to believe in the value of consumption as an intellectual ideal. We all understand that they have come to school to acquire a specific body of knowledge and to get good jobs; what goes without saying is that they, and we before them, need to acquire that specific knowledge in order to assume predetermined roles as right-thinking citizens, voters, and taxpayers. As Shoshana Felman has pointed out, most classrooms are set up to facilitate the transmission of a coherent body of information, of what she calls "ready-made knowledge," from one person, the "master," to a group of others who do not possess that information. Most classrooms thus repeat the structure of the master/slave relation I described above and in the process encourage students' belief in their own responsibility to achieve an authority similar to the teacher's. They do not, of course, actually want to become teachers, because they know what our real cultural status is as measured by our incomes, what we are capable of *owning*. What they do want is to experience the only sort of authority they know much about, which we seem to be enacting yet again in the rarefied atmospheres of our classrooms: the sort that derives from having something that others do not and that requires, depends on, those somehow inferior others.

The pattern that students discover in Barthes' analyses also suggests to them where they might begin to find their own opportunities for social analysis and for a different kind of writing. They too can look for the gap, the disguised contradiction in apparently sensible social phenomena. People who work hard, for example, do not always get rewarded with the money that they supposedly deserve; people with money have not always earned it as we like to think they should have if they are to deserve it. Sororities and fraternities "create" social opportunities and coherence in great part only by excluding other social possibilities. Students already "know" many of these things, but there seems to be no place for such knowledge in the normal contexts where they find themselves. If we can provide a place for such "inappropriate" knowledge to exist and multiply itself as analytic consideration, we provide real educational opportunities for our students that simply are not being provided in most other places in the college or university.

It is not just in reading Barthes' analyses of specific social mythologies that students can ask questions of their world, however. What we hope to teach them is not just that things are not always or exactly what they seem, but that a real conversation with social texts is possible only when we take on the responsibility of actively engaging them; only then can we figure out the "something else" that these texts attempt *not* to convey to us. We have to listen, read, and write "against the grain" of commonsense, what we all know and understand, to make that interchange possible. The usefulness of such a model for analysis lies in the potential for dialogue it establishes between a writer and the texts he or she reads and writes, whether that "text" is a piece of literature, an essay, an advertisement, a form of entertainment, or a social institution.

Of course, one could argue that we do not need Roland Barthes in the composition classroom to teach the kinds of things I have talked about here: good close reading of the New Critical kind can reveal gaps or contradictions in more or less traditional texts with or without the Marxist implications in Barthes' work. And that much is true. But there is something to be said for making our own interpretive habits and assumptions—Marxist or otherwise— clear to students, not necessarily to politicize the classroom, but to reveal that it is and has always been a political space dedicated to political activities. As Louis Althusser argues, it is the "reigning ideology of the School" to represent itself "as a neutral environment purged of ideology . . . where teachers respectful of the 'conscience' and 'freedom' of the children who are entrusted to them . . . open up for them the path to the freedom, morality and responsibility of adults by their own example, by knowledge, literature and their 'liberating' virtues" (156–57). If the space of the classroom is already filled with politics—with unspoken lessons about power and authority—then we would do well to take as our topic of consideration the "what-goes-without-saying" of our own enterprise. Barthes' essay on toys makes it possible for students to begin to see that nothing in their worlds is "neutral" or objective, the classroom and college curricula included. And what theory lets *us* do explicitly, and therefore responsibly, is address the way our own values are motivated, not natural, and thus subject to reflection, analysis, and sometimes revision.

Works Cited

Althusser, Louis. *Lenin and Philosophy and Other Essays.* Trans. Ben Brewster. New York: Monthly Review P, 1971.

Barthes, Roland. *Image–Music–Text*. Trans. Stephen Heath. New York: Hill, 1977.

———. *Mythologies*. Trans. Annette Lavers. New York: Hill, 1972.

Felman, Shoshana. "Psychoanalysis and Education: Teaching Terminable and Interminable." *Yale French Studies:* 63 (1982): 21–44

Miller, J. Hillis. "Composition and Decomposition." *Composition and Literature: Bridging the Gap*. Ed. Winifred Bryan Horner. Chicago: U of Chicago P, 1983. 38–56.

6

Teaching Common Sense: Barthes and the Rhetoric of Culture

Patricia Donahue

In a time of shifting educational paradigms and commitments, the role of the writing instructor is hard to define. Who are we? Whom do we serve? Are we responsible for teaching students the conventions of normative prose so they can communicate effectively? Should we place power—its conditions, suppressions, and disclosures—in the center of the writing course? Or should we become Socratic midwives who demonstrate, through conversation and written commentary, the collaborative and dynamic process of the production of meaning?

The third option is widely embraced by many compositionists today, and some, like Edward M. White, attempt to justify it theoretically by borrowing the vocabulary of poststructuralism. For example, in "Post-Structural Literary Criticism and the Response to Student Writing," White uses the poststructuralist term *misreading* to explain what teachers do when they examine student work and intervene in a student's writing process. White says that writing teachers, like poststructuralists, construct what they see, interpret it, by emphasizing some textual patterns instead of others and by looking

A version of this essay, entitled "Misreading Students' Texts," appeared in *Reader,* no. 17 (Spring 1987): 1–12, and is incorporated in this volume by permission.

through words to their textual unsaid (the not-yet-articulated ideas). The teacher's role, White suggests, is to uncover this unsaid, to help students discover what they *really* want to say, and to encourage students to express their authentic selves. As he explains, the teacher trusts the "intuitions of what the student meant to say or . . . what the student *could* say if he or she followed the best insights of the text . . . . insights not yet present on the page" (191). For White, the teacher brings to the classroom the best insights of contemporary theory—the knowledge that meaning is a collaborative product of both readers and writers—as well as the belief promulgated by the so-called process pedagogy that students deserve frequent and personal guidance.

Whatever its virtues, this model of instruction—this conception of the writing teacher as both a poststructuralist and a facilitator—is limited. It ignores the influences exerted by culture and discourse upon teaching and learning. Teachers are not spirit-channelers who uncover hidden intentions by suspending their judgment. They are practioners of a discipline who value "good" prose and are eager to help students "write well." Likewise, "original" writing is not an expression of authentic selfhood but a stylistic practice. In fact, we may not even want students to write "authentically"—to write what they think. As writers ourselves, we know that language speaks through us. We have "ghostwriters" who use our pens and typewriters to produce the "already said," rewritings of cultural themes and "big" ideas. The efforts of all writers are shaped by cultural forces that are beyond their control. And while we may sometimes want students to "write" their culture, rehearse its commonplaces, we may also want them to read against cultural norms. This kind of misreading hears the wild dialogue inscribed within language and addresses difference, not coherence; plurality, not consistency; representation, not intention. The teacher who performs it understands the "fact of socialness"—understands that the classroom is a social space and that ideology, point of view, and culture are inescapable. In this essay, I will examine this "fact of socialness" by using Roland Barthes' essay "The Third Meaning" as a model for a "social" pedagogy.

Barthes' Reading Process

For a model of how teachers can become aware of, and thus help students recognize, writing as cultural and identity as discursively constituted (consciously and unconsciously), Roland Barthes' essay "The Third Meaning" is useful. Analyzing film, Barthes defines an interpretive method that I have used in my freshman writing courses to teach a process of conceptual revision as well as to design writing assignments. Working through Barthes' reading stages can help students understand that "common sense" is not common at all and that all writing is socially imbricated.

In "The Third Meaning," Barthes examines several stills from Sergei Eisenstein's film *Ivan the Terrible,* and he identifies in them three layers of meaning—"informational," "symbolic," and "obtuse"—that are products of different reading strategies. These reading strategies do not represent successively better interpretive moves. There is "progress" in Barthes' model, but only in dialogical rather than linear terms. That is, each level of meaning suggests a revision of another level. Recursivity is built in. Consequently, this model can complement, even supplement, the theories of writing currently favored in our profession, theories that—in any of their many incarnations—affirm the importance of revising, reseeing, and reconceptualizing.

The "informational" level, Barthes explains, includes a film's (or text's) tangible details—what is "there" without question. "This level is communication," Barthes says. "Were it necessary to find a mode of analysis for it, I should turn to the first semiotics (that of the 'message')" (52). In film, these details consist of scenery, setting, or costume; in written texts, they consist of dialogue, plot, or denotation. The reader simply "finds" this information and identifies the "facts."

Having identified this bedrock of material, the reader begins to interpret it, although at this point in the process he or she may think that this is not interpreting at all, but merely pointing out the obvious. This second level of meaning—the reproduction of the obvious—is called the "symbolic" by Barthes. It emerges when the reader assigns symbolic, thematic meaning to information, organizing details into a new story rooted in culture and belonging to a general repertoire of ideas, a "kind of common general lexicon of symbols" (54). This reading practice is traditional and formalistic, usually taught to high-school students, and emphasizes morals and themes. If encouraged to use their preexisting repertoire to analyze a complex text like "The Fall of the House of Usher," students will often generate a conclusion like the following: madness leads to destruction and death; therefore, madness must be avoided at all costs (and can be avoided through rational action).

As this example suggests, symbolic reading is reductive. Conse-

quently, a reader has the opportunity to take another look, to revise what first seemed obvious. The meaning generated by this interpretive reworking is the *third* meaning, labeled the "obtuse" by Barthes. It is idiosyncratic, difficult to identify. Barthes first calls it the "one 'too many,' the supplement that my intellection cannot succeed in absorbing" (54). It is "not in the language-system" (60). It is a "counter-narrative" (63). In other words, the "obtuse" meaning is not in the text (it is not information) but is generated by a reader using the text to challenge the universality of the symbolic meaning and to question common sense as seamless, inviolate truth. It is a product of reading, a reader's construction. For example, a reader wanting to examine "The Fall of the House of Usher" from an "obtuse" perspective could return to it, selecting new details and using them to contradict and destabilize the symbolic theme he or she generated earlier. An "obtuse" conclusion might be drawn from the "fact" that Roderick has an invidious influence upon the narrator (he "infects" him) and that the narrator has a similar effect upon the reader (he "infects" us), contradicting the idea that madness can be controlled—there is no escape, no point outside, no alternative to sanity. Once the boundary between madness and sanity is challenged in this way, the authority of the symbolic meaning is diminished, and it becomes only one of many possible interpretations of the text, one which represents a historically conditioned value (since the sixteenth century we have excluded madness, kept it "outside") rather than a universal value.

Barthes' essay, in short, asks that we first identify information, then describe the "already said" (symbolic, normative, or cultural meanings), and finally challenge the idea of "natural" meaning by exposing *all* meaning as cultural artifacts, as icons. We can translate this method into the classroom idiom, into pedagogy, and use it to design asignments and to comment upon student writing as real writing, as a complex recoding of a social story. To describe such a pedagogy is the function of the next section.

Barthes in the Classroom

Following Barthes, I wanted my students, first, to identify textual information and, second, to assign symbolic significance to it. To accomplish these ends, I designed two assignments. The first consisted of simple questions about the text we were reading, "The Fall of the House of Usher," like "Why did the narrator visit Roderick

Usher?" and "What is a tarn?" (Because this story is puzzling, hard to pin down, my students sometimes had difficulty establishing an irrefutable level of "fact." As anyone who uses Barthes' approach will discover, locating "information" often becomes an interpretive act.) Having searched the text with this aim, students had material to "symbolize." To tease out this symbolic repertoire, I asked for an essay that would respond to the following question: "What mystery is the narrator trying to solve?" I wanted to use the students' responses as evidence of the pervasiveness of common sense.

Their responses, not surprisingly, were discursively rich. For example, none of my students argued that the narrator never solved the mystery, for mysteries they assumed, or had been told, are always solved. And the wording of the assignment even reinforced that expectation by juxtaposing the "mystery" with "solution." For other students, "mystery" signified a literary genre, and so they examined the story as a conventional mystery by asking questions like "Who killed Madeline?" and "Who killed Roderick?" In most mysteries, after all, there is a corpse to consider. In sharing the detective spirit, they assembled clues, established a motive, and collected evidence. Other students also assumed that the story was a mystery but believed that it did not require interpretation: a form of popular writing, of entertainment, mysteries (unlike "serious" genres) need not be "analyzed to death." These students reduced the story to the following narrative: a weird man attempts to rescue a sick friend and gets more than he bargained for (there is some truth to the idea, but not all readers would close down the interpretive activity at that point). Other students knew nothing about mysteries but did know a great deal about the Stephen King style of horror film, and so they looked for recognizable devices and cinematic tricks: a bloodthirsty, sex-starved female zombie and the special effects of a raging storm. Finally, some students had a smattering of psychological knowledge that they put to good use by transforming the story into a psychological puzzle. For them, the hint of incest was central and deserved attention.

My students' writing was subtended by many, often competing, cultural symbols. Barthes classifies symbolic reading into different types, and I found evidence of several: institutional symbols (thematizing the difference between serious and popular writing, the power of authority, the range of ideas acceptable in college essays); generic symbols (the constraints placed upon our reading of mysteries and horror films); and psychological symbols (the power of taboo). By identifying symbols, students began to understand that they had

been "written" by the cultural ghostwriter, that they had unconsciously reproduced obvious themes, and that discourses are highly
stratified.

To demonstrate how students were able to use their knowledge
about cultural discourses to revise content—to resee the obvious—I
will first discuss Dennis' writing. Here is the opening paragraph of
his essay, before revision:

> In Poe's famous mystery, "The Fall of the House of Usher,"
> Poe struggles with the conflict of rationality versus irratio-
> nality. In the introduction, he uses logic in determining
> why the house unnerves him. This is the mystery. He tries
> to change his view of the house by looking at its reflection,
> but this only reaffirms his first ideas of the dilapidated
> structure. When Poe enters the house, he becomes more
> superstitious and attempts to find a cause he doesn't find.
> He solves the mystery at the end of the story by making
> the house fall down.

Several of Dennis' statements revealed the thematizing and symbolizing impulse at work. For example, Dennis identifies Poe with
the narrator. Possibly he had never been told that narrators mediate
vision. Since our culture values authorship and the writing of great
men—and he seems to have adopted that value (implied in his phrase
"Poe's famous mystery")—he suggests that all writing reflects an
author's personal and unique vision. He also calls the opening of the
story the "introduction." He might have learned in high school that
introductions present a main idea and a thesis, a problem and solution. And if Dennis had that expectation, he would then skim the
story's opening paragraphs looking for a clear exposition of the problem. Furthermore, in following the guidelines of the assignment,
Dennis identifies a problem in the story—"Poe" is unnerved and tries
to control himself—a problem that he calls the "mystery." But this
mystery seems to lack a solution: "Poe's" trick fails. Since the wording of the assignment implies that a solution can be found (and
certainly assignments have a discourse of their own), Dennis tries
to find one, and so he turns to the end of the story, the place where
solutions usually appear (certainly in detective stories, and in the
particular course I am describing, we studied several examples).
Before he states a solution, however, he writes the following phrase:
"the conflict of rationality versus irrationality." "Conflict" is a term
used in high-school literature anthologies, books that introduce and

authorize thematic reading practices. "Rationality" and "irrationality" are familiar oppositions, natural-seeming binaries that control dangerous experience by containing it rhetorically.

Numerous cultural discourses—literary, institutional, generic—are presented in Dennis' writing and sometimes at odds with each other. Dennis' thinking is inconsistent at times, controlled by "shoulds" (where solutions "should" be found; what literature papers "should" talk about) and unquestioned ideas (problems have solutions). To integrate product with process, to revise his writing by revising his content (his level of discourse), he had to recognize the languages that controlled him, to *see* his assumptions. In conference, we examined his interpretive choices. It is difficult, without using transcripts, to represent the dynamics of a conference. In a general and inexact way, let me say that I ignored technique and grammatical expertise (we did not discuss sentence errors or coherence). I said nothing about the source of his ideas (literature anthologies, the high-school classroom, television). I started where he was, addressed his content: why did he classify the story as a "famous mystery," why did he refer to the conflict between "rationality" and "irrationality," why did he assume that mysteries had solutions? He first replied that some ideas were "obvious": everyone knew them. Dennis thought that "English" papers had to say certain things, be "philosophical," hard to follow. He had "thrown in" particular phrases to sound "smart." However, once he began to identify the "obvious" as such, he was able to see in his writing the same symbolic meanings that he had seen in "The Fall of the House of Usher" and in other students' papers. And that was an important move for him to make. In order to understand—and thus modify—his discursive choices, he had to read his essay as a "real" text, like Poe's. Then he could revise his content. His revision looked like this:

> In "The Fall of the House of Usher," the narrator struggles with the conflict of rationality versus irrationality. In the opening paragraph, he uses logic to determine why the house unnerves him. He tries to change his view of the house by looking at its reflection, but this only reaffirms his first ideas of the dilapidated structure. When the narrator enters the house, he becomes more superstitious and attempts to find a reason, but does not succeed.

From the "obvious," Dennis turns to an alternative heuristic—the "problematic." He refers to the "narrator" rather than "Poe," eliminating his earlier reference to the value of the story. He adopts one of the conventions of the college writing course—assuming the importance of the material being written about. He substitutes the term "opening paragraph" for "introduction." He no longer expects the story to "introduce" a problem in its opening pages or to solve in it in final pages. "The Fall of the House of Usher" is a different kind of story for Dennis now, a mystery without a solution. But there is one change Dennis does not make. He does not clarify the issue of "conflict." Perhaps it is one symbolism he believes he can control.

The goal of my second assignment was to give the symbolic free expression so students could begin to identify what they bring to the reading and writing activity, and to discover that the processing of information depends upon many cultural givens. At this point in the course, they had naturalized their interpretations, made sense of the story, by translating details into familiar themes—the greatness of Poe as a writer, the conflict between sanity and insanity. For them to experiment fully with a Barthesian approach, they could not stop there. They had to press on and become "obtuse" readers of a sort. (I realize that there is some irony in my use of the word *obtuse* in this context, for we often think that students are aggravatingly obtuse when they discuss literature in ways that make good sense to them, if not to us.)

To encourage my students to become obtuse readers, I designed a third assignment that asked them to look a second time at the essays they had just written (the answer to the question, "What mystery is the narrator trying to solve?"). They were to identify a significant repetition in *their essays,* something they had repeated several times. They were then to answer the following questions, again in essay form. First, why did you repeat this point? And, second, are there other details in the story you could have discussed at length? What are they, and what would you have said about them? In this assignment, I wanted to stress several points: first, that the essay about "mystery" was an interpretation, accomplishing the simultaneous highlighting and deemphasizing of textual information; second, that students could examine the text obtusely by rereading it, by rewriting it, and by revising their understanding of its details; and third, that their own writing was interpretable—a web of significant connections and displacements.

This assignment, in short, asked them to resee their ideas and, again, through the process of writing revise the actual content. Let us look at another example of student writing, this time Marita's.

"For a moment she remained trembling and reeling to and fro . . . [she] bore him to the floor a corpse, and a victim to the terrors he had anticipated. . . . I saw the mighty walls rushing asunder . . . and the deep and dark tarn at my feet closed sullenly and silently over the fragments of the House of Usher." This incident, where soon after Roderick Usher is killed, the house destructs, becomes one of several examples of repetition Poe uses to reveal the connections between Usher's family and the house in which they inhabit. Other repetitions, I believe, include words, ideas, and moods, that help the readers make sense of the story on the basis of this connection. However, these repetitions, I believe, create other repetitions to remain unaccounted for because of the nature of those repetitions in his description.

Asked to discuss repetitions in her own work and to examine her patterns of selection, Marita analyzes the story's repetitions rather than her own. Possibly she was not able to regard her own work as interpretable or to ignore the internal voice (the cultural censor) that labels student writing as nonwriting. To respond to her essay as a genuine example of personal and collective inquiry, I used Barthes' vocabulary—informational, symbolic, and obtuse. As information, I marked summaries of the text, statements that few readers would challenge (for example, the idea that Roderick Usher is killed and the house is destroyed) so that Marita would know what she had identified as facts or givens. I also marked symbolic meanings: personal symbolisms (features of the writer's personal idiom—Marita, for instance, writes "I believe" to alert the reader that she is making an important point), literary symbolism (terms from literary criticism like "mood"), and rhetorical symbolism (the convention of introducing an essay with a quotation). In addition, I read against the emphasis of Marita's writing, identifying contradictions and the play of similarity (repetitions and coordinate statements) and difference (subordinate statements)—I read obtusely. For example, Marita presents the quotation as a significant repetition but never explains why she thinks it is significant or how Poe specifically uses it. She says that repetitions "create other repetitions," but does not explain her point. On one hand, she wants to discuss the "mystery" of Poe's use of repetition. On the other hand, her repetition of the term "repetition" and her emphasis upon "connections" creates a tautology. It occurred to me that she had employed a model of thesis and support that emphasized unity rather than difference and prevented her from presenting two perspectives side-by-side. (Even though I had this "intuition," I did not share it with her. I wanted to look at rather than through her text.) In general, I told Marita what I saw in her writing—her acceptance of specific details as noninterpretable "facts," her use of conventions, her contradictions. Her writing about Poe's text was, in turn, a text to be read and written about. As we can see from both examples of student writing, Barthes' process can help teachers and students situate *all* writing as a map of culture.

Barthes in Composition

There are several points about Barthes' essay that I want to separate out in this last section. By borrowing its conceits, students can transform themselves into obtuse readers who resist the unconscious reproduction of common sense and familiar truths. They can also resist classifying themselves as "novices" who never write as well as the "experts" and whose texts represent a second and less valuable order of language—pseudodiscourse. Barthes' method can also be used to challenge the distinction between process and product that dominates our thinking about writing. "Process" continues to command the attention of the profession, as if students write about nothing, out of nothing. But if we do indeed want students to revise their material in comprehensive and meaningful ways—as we so often claim—students will need to examine their content carefully, and we will need to help them. The question then is how to encourage students to see their material differently without implicitly or explicitly demanding that they reproduce our opinions and points of view (a problem that mars the otherwise useful *Reading Texts* by Kathleen McCormick, Gary Waller, and Linda Flower).

This issue of reproduction, which finally is an issue of power, touches upon a related concern—the right of students to their own language, a position widely held by compositionists these days. If students have this right, then our responsibility as teachers may very well be to intuit their intentions, to help them say what they *really* want to say. But Barthes would approach this issue differently. For Barthes, appropriation is inevitable. All readers bring assumptions and expectations to the task. We cannot follow our students' sentences without comparing them to other sentences we have read. We cannot follow the development of an idea without evaluating it. Furthermore, we do our students little good by suggesting that there exists a transcendent realm where authentic expression is found. Students do not have "their own language." They have *languages,* multiple languages—the teacher's discourse, an institution's discourse, Poe's discourse, and if we teach it, Barthes' discourse as well.

This last point returns us to the issue, stated in my opening paragraph, of roles and responsibilities. If we use Barthes' method, we will become critics of culture who demystify the social machinery. And his essay even provides a script for this role, instructions we can follow to read the classroom as a cultural site, to define writing as a social practice, and to identify student writing as legitimate writing. But at the same time that Barthes' essay shows us how to read culture, it also suggests that no position, even its own, is ideologically "safe" or neutral. Barthes' work offers only one way of seeing. In adopting its language, or the language of any theoretical text, we do not avoid the struggle to know. In fact, using theory means accepting responsibility for the knowledge we "always already" have. And an important aspect of that responsibility is examining our biases: how discipline shapes practice; how power is distributed and released in the classroom; and how our informed conception of "effective" writing shares our response to student writing. In other words, in teaching cultural critique, we must not become blind to the ideology of our own position, or to the fact that understanding the nature of discursive constraints does not release us from discourse or ideology. At best (and this is a great deal), we may be able to frame new discourses that challenge traditional channels of thought. But even these new discourses are not "extradiscursive." And when reading Barthes, when using a theoretical text to rewrite the pedagogical scene, we do well to keep that idea in mind.

Works Cited

Barthes, Roland. "The Third Meaning." *Image–Music–Text.* Trans. Stephen Heath. New York: Hill, 1977. 52–68.

McCormick, Kathleen, Gary Waller, and Linda Flower. *Reading Texts: Reading, Responding, Writing.* Lexington, MA: Heath, 1987.

White, Edward M. "Post-Structural Literary Criticism and the Response to Student Writing." *College Composition and Communication* 35 (1984): 186–95.

7

Bakhtin's Rhetoric

Jon Klancher

Teaching "critical thinking" today often means teaching a form of ideological analysis based on models forged by Kenneth Burke or Roland Barthes, Marx or Freud. These models have shared a common procedure: the interpreter starts with the readable surface of a text and works purposefully toward its ideological core. In Marx's view or Burke's, ideological motives control political or aesthetic discourses; Barthes shows us how the historicity of a culture is disguised by the rhetorics of nature. But these important forms of ideological analysis were developed in order to criticize the widely held belief in a universally valid rational discourse that all readers and writers understood. The great masters of ideological interpretation assumed such a belief when they revealed that disguised power and hidden interests—those of class, race, gender—exert a decisive control over the apparently "democratic" world of reading and writing. Today it appears that students are increasingly immune to the surprises of such ideological discoveries. But this may be less because of a so-called new conservatism among students than because, unlike many of their teachers, they have never fully credited the belief in a universally shared public language that represents all our collective interests.[1]

This helps explain the attraction of those newer forms of critical or ideological analysis that do not begin by assuming a common world of public language, but rather an already-divided, conflictual, and contested scene of social languages or "discursive practices." Mikhail Bakhtin's "dialogic" rhetoric is surely one of the most significant of these, and here I want to explore the challenge that Bakhtin's work poses to some basic notions we have about reading and writing "in public." Bakhtin's work suggests a kind of ideological analysis that does not proceed immediately from "surface" to "depth," but rather moves laterally across texts, to identify the "social languages" that weave among them. A Bakhtinian pedagogy would show how these social languages can be found and articulated within what otherwise appears as a largely univocal or "monologic" sphere of public discourse. But I will not offer a simple classroom technique in which Bakhtin's method can be straightforwardly "applied." Composition pedagogy today is thick with techniques and technical solutions. Bakhtin's expansive cultural scope begs technical solutions to narrowly defined problems and invites us to redefine certain basic matters of writing and teaching themselves.

Rhetoric, Persuasion, and Trope

Bakhtin's writings suggest a new meaning for the concept of rhetoric because they refuse the great modern (and postmodern) division between "language" and "ideology." Nietzsche once distinguished "rhetoric-as-trope" from "rhetoric-as-persuasion," but from the beginning the Bakhtin circle spurned this opposition and what it would come to imply. Along with his colleagues V. N. Voloshinov and P. N. Medvedev, Bakhtin developed in the 1920s a sociolinguistic and critical response to the determinist theories of language put forward by Ferdinand de Saussure and Joseph Stalin. Against their views that language-acts are determined by supervising structures (economic or linguistic), Bakhtin and Voloshinov developed a situational model of language that accentuates the social and concrete character of practical speech "acts."[2] Bakhtin himself refuses to speak of "language" as a totalized entity. Languages are multiple and they entail thinking agents:

> The actively literary linguistic consciousness at all times and everywhere comes upon "languages" and not language. Consciousness finds itself inevitably facing the necessity of *having to choose a language*. With each literary-verbal performance, consciousness must actively orient

itself amidst heteroglossia, it must move in and occupy a
position for itself within it, it chooses, in other words, a
"language."[3]

Bakhtin's crucial starting point—the diversity of practical languages rather than a unitary abstract structure—leads him to argue
that every effort to impose unity on these languages is "monologic."
The institutions of the school, the state, and the church enforce
monologic languages as the voice of culture, the voice of authority,
the voice of God ventriloquized through the literary critic, the politi-
cian, or the priest. His terms *dialogic* and *monologic* thus describe
the uses of language rather than inherent properties of language
itself.

By embracing both figurative and ideological gestures, Bakhtin's
notion of rhetoric challenges both our prevailing commonsense understanding of that term and the more recent deconstructive sense
of rhetoric made influential by Paul de Man. The commonly taught
model of rhetoric posits a writer directly addressing a reader, antici-
pating his or her responses and deflecting his or her objections in the
effort of "persuasion." To counter this naïve model, Paul de Man
recalled Nietzsche's *aporia* between rhetoric-as-trope and rhetoric-
as-persuasion[4] to stress the figurative "turn" that tropes take away
from communicated meaning—thus immobilizing rhetoric as a social
or persuasive agent. But Bakhtin—whose influence de Man warned
against in one of his last talks[5]—essentially reverses the relation
between the persuasive and troping powers of rhetoric. The diverse
meanings of the trope do not prevent it from "meaning" any one
thing, but rather signal the interference of one intended meaning by
another meaning that deflects it or crosses its path. Bakhtin thus
recognizes "indeterminacy" as a sociopolitical rather than a linguistic condition:

> The word, directed toward its object, enters a dialogically
> agitated and tension-filled environment of alien words,
> value judgments and accents, weaves in and out of com-
> plex interrelationships, merges with some, recoils from
> others, intersects with yet a third group: and all this may
> crucially shape discourse, may leave a trace in all its
> semantic layers, may complicate its expression and influ-
> ence its entire stylistic profile.[6]

It is this interference, this "tension-filled environment of alien
words," that a monologic language attempts to suppress. The diver-

sity of social languages Bakhtin called "heteroglossia"—or "verbal-ideological points of view"—appear in the novel, parody, and certain forms of popular literature. But the idea of heteroglossia depends finally on a notion of rhetoric in which figurations and ideological intentions collide.

For in fact the simple rhetorical model of "persuasion" (writer-message-reader) taught in schools was already a monologic model, and in this sense Bakhtin shares de Man's suspicion of the utilitarian rhetorics that have dominated pedagogy since the late eighteenth century. But unlike de Man, Bakhtin reads the dictionary as a social text—the diverse meanings of a particular trope form a "spectral dispersion in an atmosphere filled with the alien words, value judgments and accents through which the ray passes on its way toward the object" (*The Dialogic Imagination* 277). Hence the choice between rhetoric-as-persuasion and rhetoric-as-trope is no choice at all. That which "persuades" does so either by suppressing the diversity of social languages (heteroglossia) or by clarifying them—in other words, by a politics of figurative language as such.

Paraphrase, Parody, Style

All this is to suggest that Bakhtin's arguments will be most useful not if they are simply "applied" in the writing classroom, but rather if they help us rethink its purpose and its major functions. Here the aim is not only to improve students' "skills"—as the technocratic conception of the writing course has influentially defined it—but also to empower students to master the monologues of which they have become hapless and usually ineffective reproducers. To foreshorten a potentially lengthy survey of such pedagogic remodelling, I will briefly focus on two cornerstones of standard rhetorical instruction.

Invoking Authority

To the dualist model of reader/writer, Bakhtin adds a third voice who participates in, or interferes with, the relation of reader to writer. The most explicit version of this third voice appears as what Voloshinov called "reported speech"—what we would otherwise call citation, quotation, and paraphrase.[7] The writer's effort to enlist authorities is an essential yet hazardous enterprise, since the reader can also interpret such authorities against the writer's intent. Not only the quoted or paraphrased words of the third party must be figured into the dialogue, but also his or her context and motives.

Further, quoting, paraphrasing, or citing introduces an explicitly hierarchical dynamic into the dialogue—the third party becomes either more or less authoritative than the writer. Voloshinov associates the strategies of such reported speech with institutional discourses and speech situations that overtly entail power—as any academic who acquires these essential tools knows very well. It is worth recalling here how much difficulty students have getting this right. Using quotation, citation, and paraphrase properly—that is, according to norms of academic prose—is perhaps the most awkwardly learned of writing skills. It exposes students to the complex social and cultural relations of language that comprise "university discourse."

But the most useful notion here is Voloshinov's idea of "paraphrase," where the writer's own language reshapes the cited authority's language and dialogically grapples with it (e.g., "She says that . . ."). The inevitable misrepresentation of paraphrase is a strategic transfer of power, the staging of one voice by another that absorbs it and still marks its difference from the writer's. As it departs from quotation, periphrasis introduces an irreversible element of *parody* into the writer's language. In the case of student writing, this parodic tone often remains unconscious or at least inexplicit, but I suspect that the kind of writing many of us reward with an "A" is the kind that recognizes and boldly accentuates the parodic intention that most students suppress in fear of censure.

Strikingly, then, Voloshinov's and Bakhtin's local strategies of dialogic engagement form an arc that extends from a simple citation of authority on the one hand to a complex, subversive engagement against received authority in the periphrastic texture of prose style itself. In his later work, Bakhtin bridges rhetoric and literary fiction by accentuating parody as turning another speaker's language against itself. Writing parodically means populating another's language with one's own intentions, what Bakhtin calls "verbal masquerade" or "not talking straight." In a well-known essay on black literature, Henry Louis Gates identifies parody with what has long been called, in American black culture, "signifying." Signifying—an explicitly social parody of one dominant culture by a subjugated culture—reenacts Hegel's master-slave dialectic in the realm of discourse. It empties out the discourse of mastery by mimicking it.[8] Parody thus becomes the chief mode of resistance to power for those who cannot find alternative ground on which to stand. Parody flouts the master's language by exaggerating its gestures—or, in Bakhtin's terms, by inhabiting the language of the lords with the intentions of the peasants.[9]

The importance of parody is usually lost in literary instruction that makes it a mere imitation of style without the pointed edge of more dramatic ironical modes like satire (e.g., as in a parody of Faulkner's or Hemingway's style). But Bakhtin will argue that all self-consciously "dialogic" discourses are fundamentally parodic whether they make parodic intentions explicit or not. This is why a writer like Dostoyevsky—hardly an obvious choice of comic writer— serves Bakhtin and Voloshinov so well to demonstrate the reach of parody in dialogic discourse:

> Once in winter, on a cold and frosty evening—very late evening, rather, it being already the twelfth hour—three *extremely distinguished* gentlemen were sitting in a *comfortable,* even *sumptuously appointed,* room inside a *handsome* two-story house on Petersburg Island and were occupied in *weighty and superlative* talk on an *extremely remarkable* topic. All three gentlemen were officials of the rank of general. They were seated around a small table, each in a *handsome* upholstered chair, and during pauses in the conversation they *comfortably* sipped champagne. (Voloshinov's italics)[10]

As Voloshinov points out, this passage appears "stylistically wretched and banal." But Dostoyevsky's stylistic disjointedness, like Theodore Dreiser's, signals to Bakhtin the presence of dialogic parody that resists monologic mastery. In the passage above, the terms *comfortable, handsome, extremely distinguished, sumptuously appointed, and weighty and superlative* belong not to the narrator but to his parody of the language of the government officials he is portraying. This is often subtle in so-called "realist" fiction, but overtly heteroglot parody has become the unmistakable signature of the more fiercely dialogized fictions of postmodernism—those of William Burroughs or Thomas Pynchon or Don DeLillo.

To reveal the parodic trope within the periphrastic gesture is to confront the open struggle of authoritative and subversive voices. Voloshinov's mechanics of "reported speech" and Bakhtin's late work on fictional dialogic parody belong together, and it seems to me they suggest a pedagogy whose aim is to disengage student writers from crippling subservience to the received languages they grapple with. This remains a general rather than a social and political matter until such languages can be identified and situated, as I will argue shortly below. But one caveat concerning parody should be mentioned now. Bakhtin's influential work on Rabelaisian parody implied that the laughter of parody is inherently subversive of authoritative discourses. Perhaps in the early Renaissance it was. But the very briefest survey of postmodern culture shows that today parody is a generalized discourse that features a *countersubversive parody,* namely the language of the mass media that echoes, contains, and abolishes the subversive intentions of subcultural discourses. For us, parody is a generalized linguistic currency through which a great many political and social intentions are presently being expressed. For this reason, we should not assign some inherent political meaning to this or that discursive mode (as in "parody vs. talking straight"), but rather try to identify the social positioning of contemporary languages, and thus lead students toward some leverage upon their political strategies and monologic effects. To this end, it seems necessary to concentrate on two institutional centers where current discourses are fashioned, tested, and distributed—the mass media and "university discourse." Again, I will approach this question through a traditional rhetorical category: the hierarchy of styles.

Official and Subcultural Styles

The old rhetorical distinctions among "high," "middle," and "low" styles survive today as a remnant in handbooks of modern rhetoric, usually classified under the rubric *diction.* For our purpose, such traditional terms need to be translated into terms that refer to official,"plain," and subcultural styles. The high or official style is often the style of institutional power, its terms drawn from such institutional voices as police reports, hospital communiqués, or government announcements, and diffused to us through the six-o'clock news.[11] At the other end lie the dialects of contemporary subcultures—some dominated, like black urban culture, and some the mirror image of dominant official culture, like the underworld language that provides colorful if rather insignificant examples of the "low" style. Most handbooks of rhetoric provide accessible vocabulary keys to the markers of the official, middle or "plain," and colloquial or subcultural styles. Translating plain terms into their official and subcultural variants is often an entertaining demonstration for students in the classroom, and the lesson that often flows from this demonstration is that good writers prefer the "middle" style and become conscious enough of archly "high" or "low" styles that they only use such styles deliberately, for comic or demonstrative effect. The lesson usually ends here, with a prescription for an unpretentious educated plain style and a prohibition against both euphemistic official terms and subcultural dialects.

Bakhtin's rhetoric shows why this pedagogy of the "middle style" imparts the wrong lesson. For if the "official" language of police, military, and professional bureaucracies is clearly "monologic," so too is the apparently desirable "middle" style when it is presented as value-neutral, free of "bias" or "propagandistic" intent, or transparently "plain." This was particularly the claim of a Cold-War pedagogy anxious to distinguish ideological languages from a language "beyond ideology"—the aim proposed memorably by George Orwell in "Politics and the English Language." But Bakhtin's work suggests that the "middle style" becomes in fact a *language of maneuver* between the euphemistic, inflated style of officialdom and the stigmatized languages of subcultural resistance. It would be wrong, of course, to characterize subcultural styles as simply "dialogic" in the honorific sense Bakhtin's prestige has given that term. (Hence I am not suggesting a bath in the colorful waters of subcultural styles.) Quite the contrary, these apparently diverse styles are already scarred by the monologic effect of the official style. Both the official style *and* the subcultural styles are circulated and maintained by the mass media. The media uses them to provide the "schooling" in language that every writing teacher uses a classroom to confront.

The argument against a transparent, value-neutral "middle" style has been influentially made in recent works by Richard Lanham,[12] but Lanham's polemic needs to be clearly distinguished from Bakhtin's and Voloshinov's dialectic of social languages. Up to a point, Lanham shares with Bakhtin and Voloshinov the critique of "official" and "school" styles as purposeful modes of institutional domination. Lanham's "paramedic" revising method (in *Revising Prose*) is an especially useful and teachable technique of cutting through the clutter of various institutional monologues. But rather than returning students to the transparent, illusory simplicity of a "plain style," Lanham wants them to discover the rhythms of a highly personal "voice" that is not simply the expression of a classically defined "self," but rather the mobile pyrotechnics of what Richard Poirier once called "the performing self." We should "think of ourselves as actors playing social roles, a series of roles which vary with the social situation in which we find ourselves . . . the sum of all the public roles we play" (*Revising Prose* 104). But Lanham's idea of the "social" means a competitive, social Darwinist conception of social mobility and aggression that resituates the self among the new demands of a postmodern culture. Far from "critical thinking," the new stylist fashions himself or herself to survive in a postmodern situation that plays what Jean-François Lyotard calls "language games," each of which corresponds to a particular institutional demand for performance.[13] Lanham wants to preserve a "central self" sought by the old-fashioned humanism by joining it to the canny performing self who ranges among the language games, often in a parodic spirit, distinguishing himself or herself by an admirably insolent stylistic panache from the various institutionalized discourses that the deluded can only fitfully try to reproduce.

Lanham's pedagogy and Bakhtin's rhetoric both argue a parodic stance toward institutionalized languages, but Lanham's verbal performer will not really be a critic of such languages. He or she will only accommodate them by a strenuous effort to achieve personal distinction. In Bakhtin's dialectic of social languages, however, the reader/writer cannot preserve what Lanham prizes as a "central self" behind the social mask. Here it is worth recalling a formulation quoted earlier: "Consciousness finds itself inevitably facing the necessity of *having to choose a language.*" Lanham's stylistic survivor must dance among the language games to preserve a distinctive self, but Bakhtin's reader/writer must declare a position, take up and occupy a language already existing in the discourses of heteroglossia. He or she can only adopt a language that others already share, making a choice that is at once stylistic and ideological. To be "social" is not to don a range of masks or impersonate a repertoire of roles, but to declare oneself situated among the existing languages of heteroglossia. This choice means becoming aware of the ideological commitments signified by the various styles that circulate among us. It also means giving up the illusion—preserved even by so astute an observer of postmodern culture as Lanham—that the reader/writer's "self" can be defined or held apart from the conflict of social languages that constitute our individually expressed words.

Using Bakhtin's Rhetoric

Bakhtin's rhetoric identifies the contemporary fragmentation of languages as conflicting exercises of power and resistance waged in the media of discourse, visible today not only in literature but in the languages of everyday life and the composition classroom. This is why there is no real choice to make between teaching "style"—even Lanham's postmodern performer's sense of style—and teaching the discursive modes of "writing across the curriculum." This style-versus-structure division among theorists of rhetoric merely projects two ways of adapting to "things as they are"—and drains the idea of "style" itself of critical force. The postmodern performer thinks a sense of style will preserve him or her from political-social choice; the cross-curriculum theorist thinks critical thought can take place within an institutionally narrowed and defined range of acceptable "university discourse." Both want to avoid the consequences of Bakhtin's rhetoric—using language inescapably demands choice among the political and social languages of one's time.

Styles of writing and speaking signal ideological investments. Composition pedagogy might therefore begin with a wide survey of significant contemporary styles and their social-political signals. Ranging from different sorts of "official" styles to sharply defined subcultural styles, these samples will also include the kinds of *Time-Life* mass-media discourses that often echo bits and pieces of social languages within their effort to achieve a lucid "plain" style. The most effective mass-media language is typically a patchwork of official and subcultural vocabularies, archly managed with that peculiar kind of parodic tone that popular journalists use to raise themselves above the fray of social languages and thus declare their fitness to survey the contemporary social and political scene. That parodic tone—heightened by the more conservative journalists to achieve a truly countersubversive style—forms the monologic authority of mass media as it strips heteroglot languages of their specific social character. There is a paradox here well worth developing in the rhetoric course. Mass-media language circulates the fragments of social languages, a kind of hyper-heteroglossia that mysteriously re-imposes monologic authority through its extraordinary ability to absorb and neutralize the conflict of social languages. Every citation of heteroglossia by *Time* magazine uses "reported" speech to separate the social dialects from their users, to diminish the force of social languages by recirculating them at higher speed. These citations become, of course, instant clichés. They detoxify the social languages they cite and reinforce the authority of media's globalized voice. But advertisers and media magicians always need more raw material, and they are perpetually required to find new social dialects to feed into their monologic machine. So there is always the moment when the mass media must *display* the diversity of social languages and the cultural conflicts they embody. Hence mass media language remains one of the most useful indexes of how diverse social languages can be, as well as how they are destroyed.

Apart from identifying these social languages and their political charge, a rhetorical "reading" would pay special attention to the way any one text cites, paraphrases, and parodies other social languages. Writing assignments, by the same token, would ask students to "parody" one or more social styles—if by "parody" we mean not the lesser exercise of imitation, but the frankly critical, dialogically informed encounter between social languages that Bakhtin implies.[14] What these examples help suggest, more broadly, is that no one can write in a "style of one's own," and the aim of such teaching will be to reveal to students how much their own writing has been framed by particular stylistic practices they have absorbed unconsciously as monologic authority or—as one hopes—consciously as dialogic strategies.

Whatever specific techniques might be used to explore Bakhtin's rhetoric, one fact will become unavoidably clear. The academic discourse of the writing teacher constantly tends toward monologue, the voice of classroom authority. Among the social languages to be exposed to criticism and perhaps iconoclastic parody may be the pedagogue's own voice. Marx once pointedly asked who would educate the educators. Among the possible answers to that question would be Bakhtin's: the educator will be dialogized as well, exposed to the risk and surprise of heteroglot encounter. In a time when ideological mystifications appear as "second nature," the surprises of Bakhtin's rhetoric may be well worth having.

Notes

1. See, on this point, John Guillory, "Canonical and Non-Canonical."

2. See Medvedev and Bakhtin, *The Formal Method in Literary Scholarship;* Voloshinov, *Marxism and the Philosophy of Language;* and Bakhtin, *The Dialogic Imagination.*

3. Bakhtin, *The Dialogic Imagination* 295.

4. De Man, "Action and Identity in Nietzsche."

5. See de Man, "Dialogue and Dialogism." My summary of de Man's position here is so sketchy as to risk parodying his complex arguments, and it is well worth taking seriously de Man's suspicion that Bakhtin's dialogism traffics in a covert "hermeneutics" that invites a theological understanding (as, for instance, Holquist understands Bakhtin).

6. Bakhtin, *The Dialogic Imagination* 276.

7. Voloshinov, *Marxism and the Philosophy of Language* 146.

8. See Gates, "The Blackness of Blackness."

9. See *Rabelais and His World,* the most influential of Bakhtin's texts among students of early modern European history and culture.

10. Quoted in Voloshinov, *Marxism and the Philosophy of Language* 205.

11. The phrase *official style* was coined by Richard Lanham in *Revising Prose* to denote the language disseminated by official institutions. "Decedent" for "dead," "expired" for "died," and other bureaucratic terms fit here, but more importantly the meretricious euphemisms of the Vietnam War and a style heavy with abstract nominalizations, passive verbs, and strings of prepositional phrases. My analysis here is indebted to Lanham's polemic against the influence of the official style, despite criticisms to be made shortly, below.

12. *Style: An Anti-Textbook; Revising Prose;* and *Literacy and the Survival of Humanism.*

13. Lyotard, *The Postmodern Condition.*

14. Let me take a brief example from a writing course focused on American social languages since the 1960s. Among other topics, I asked students to inventory the languages of the black civil-rights writers. Not only were students unable to describe a general "style" that would include writers like Baldwin, King, Cleaver, or (for the sake of comparison) Jackson—they also could not reduce any single writer to a single rhetorical model. Students found King playing a New Testament style against a classically American political rhetoric; Baldwin adopting an Old Testament diction laced with the syntax of self-conscious literary allusiveness; Cleaver forming a "dialogue" between a selectively chosen street language and a frequently savage parody of official phrases and styles. Now any of these styles can be identified through a "close reading" of these writers' stylistic tactics. But viewed relationally or dialogically rather in terms of a static rhetorical model, these strategies take on a new interest insofar as they compose a sociopolitical field of choices and tactics with particular investments. The civil rights movement itself stopped appearing to students as a historical monolith. For along with the dialogue of languages within these writers also appears the evolving conflicts within ideas and political stances (Christian/Muslim, questions of political vs. economic equality, choices of national and discursive traditions, division among audiences of civil-rights movement discourse, etc.). For purposes of comparison, I asked students to examine Jesse Jackson's language of the 1980s. Here they did not, as I had expected, simply find some new version of languages they had al-

ready found at work in black writers of the sixties. Instead they found that what distinguishes Jackson's language from his predecessors' is the way he incorporates, by allusion or parody, the *consumer culture* into a black public language. His style dialogizes (and remains politically critical toward) the discourse of mass culture that American blacks have entered as a result of the civil-rights movement, the music industry, organized sports, and so forth. Meanwhile, Jackson's language also develops the biblical and literary allusiveness that characterized earlier black public language. The resulting Jacksonian discourse—neither wholly outside (like the later King speeches) nor wholly inside contemporary capitalist culture—reveals the cultural and political investments Jackson has made. It remains to be seen how other black languages will emerge in the public sphere as they must somehow grapple dialogically with Jackson's distinctive style.

Works Cited

Bakhtin, M. M. *The Dialogic Imagination: Four Essays*. Trans. Caryl Emerson, ed. Michael Holquist. Austin: U of Texas P, 1981.

———. *Rabelais and His World*. Trans. Helene Iswolsky. Cambridge: MIT P, 1968.

De Man, Paul. "Action and Identity in Nietzsche." *Yale French Studies* 52 (1975): 16–30.

———. "Dialogue and Dialogism." *The Resistance to Theory*. Minneapolis: U of Minnesota P, 1986. 106–14.

Gates, Henry L., Jr., "The Blackness of Blackness: A Critique of the Sign and the Signifying Monkey." *Black Literature and Literary Theory*. New York: Methuen, 1984. 285–322.

Guillory, John. "Canonical and Non-Canonical: A Critique of the Current Debate." *Journal of English Literary History* 54 (1987): 483–527.

Lanham, Richard A. *Literacy and the Survival of Humanism*. New Haven: Yale UP, 1983.

———. *Revising Prose*. New York: Scribners, 1979.

———. *Style: An Anti-Textbook*. New Haven: Yale UP, 1974.

Lyotard, Jean-François. *The Postmodern Condition: A Report on Knowledge*. Trans. Geoff Bennington and Brian Massumi. Minneapolis: U of Minnesota P, 1984.

Medvedev, P. N., and M. M. Bakhtin. *The Formal Method in Literary*

Scholarship: A Critical Introduction to Sociological Poetics. Trans. Albert J. Wehrle. Baltimore: Johns Hopkins UP, 1978.

Voloshinov, V. N. *Marxism and the Philosophy of Language*. Trans. Ladislav Matejka and I. R. Titunik. New York: Humanities P, 1973.

8

Bombs and Other Exciting Devices, or the Problem of Teaching Irony

Lori Chamberlain

Do you intend to result my passion? Is it not enough, ungrateful as you are, to make no return to all the favours I have done you; but you must treat me with ironing?
　　　　　　　　　　—Mrs. Slipslop in *Joseph Andrews*

In the representation of power, the ironing board has long served as a sign of women's work, connoting the relegation of the female to the relative powerlessness of the home. Irony, on the other hand, has traditionally been discussed as a trope of the powerful, to be mastered by the rulers of language and the state. Fielding's irony, deployed at Mrs. Slipslop's expense, depends for its comic effect on our recognition of this fact, that is, on our recognition of the incommensurability of the domains of ironing and irony. Unfortunately, the hierarchical implications of this distinction are still with us, sometimes where we might not expect them to be. Specifically, in the college writing course—the course charged with teaching the rhetoric of reading and writing—one might expect students to be empowered culturally by learning to master the trope of the powerful. Yet this is all too obviously not what occurs.

If our textbooks are any indication, few of us spend any—or any significant—time teaching irony. Those teachers who have presented an essay dependent on irony to their freshman writing classes probably already know how much difficulty students typically have in

This essay originally appeared in *College English* 51.1 (Jan. 1989): 25–36, copyright © 1989 by the National Council of Teachers of English, and is reprinted with permission.

interpreting ironic meaning. Students may miss not only the "joke" of such essays, but also their critical force. Perhaps because of this, few of us encourage students to use irony in their own writing. Following Richard Ohmann's lead in examining the politics of what we *do* teach in the writing classroom, I would like to speculate on the politics of *not* teaching irony.

For the decision to teach or not teach irony is a political gesture in a way that the decision to teach other tropes, such as metaphor, for example, is not. Irony is not simply a trope among tropes, not simply a neutral and purely formal device. Unlike other tropes, it defines a political relationship between the user and the audience being addressed or excluded. Even while provoking laughter, irony invokes notions of hierarchy and subordination, judgment and perhaps even moral superiority. It is subversive. And it challenges some of the principles of "good" writing as they are embodied in composition textbooks, particularly principles concerning clarity and sincerity. Our reluctance to teach irony may also tell us something about the relationship between teachers and students in composition classrooms, and about the relationship between a composition curriculum and the culture it serves.

A notoriously difficult trope to define and confine, irony may refer to dissonances at many levels, from the linguistic to the metaphysical. It has been defined simply as a figure of speech, more broadly as the defining principle of the novel or as the structure of all good poetry, and more globally as an attitude toward the world or as the defining structure of an age. Much of the discussion in this century has centered on problems of defining and classifying, distinguishing irony as a figure of speech from irony as a figure of thought, or dividing the term into categories: Socratic, dramatic, verbal, cosmic, romantic, single, double, unmastered, mastered, and so on. The efforts to classify it have, in fact, shown the difficulty—if not the impossibility—of "mastering" irony.

If the chief purpose of defining irony has been to clarify its meaning, another purpose has also been to restrict its power, for there are ample warnings against its dangers. In Thomas Mann's *The Magic Mountain,* for example, Settembrini provides the following cautionary words: "Irony, forsooth! Guard yourself, Engineer, from the sort of irony that thrives up here; guard yourself altogether from taking on their mental attitude! Where irony is not a direct and classic device of oratory, not for a moment equivocal to a healthy mind, it makes for depravity, it becomes a drawback to civilization, an unclean traffic with the forces of reaction, vice, and materialism" (220).

The warning is, of course, ironic, coming as it does in a novel by one of the century's best-known ironists. As D. C. Muecke (to whom I owe this example) argues, "[W]e ought to be suspicious of the general charge that irony is rocking the boat. It is the function of irony to point out that it is the waves that are doing the rocking and that this is only to be expected when one is at sea and not on dry land" (245).

But Settembrini's warning has been reiterated by those who fear that irony, like rhetoric in general, will be used to divide truth from language, and that irony in particular is capable of promoting both individual and global moral decay. In the conclusion of his 1946 study of irony and drama, for example, Alan Reynolds Thompson includes the following indictment of the role of irony in modern society:

> The cosmic despair of the late nineteenth century left a spiritual vacuum in the place of traditional religion; and into that vacuum rushed all the gaseous isms generated in our miasmatic modern society. In the anarchy that followed the First World War, these isms could take bodily shape in oppressive and revolutionary new governments. But we Americans ignored the dangers and made whoopee until we had a Depression, and a Second World War, to sober us. We might have saved ourselves and all civilization from at least the last horrible holocaust if we had a solid faith and acted on it. Instead, we descended in the 'twenties into our lowest depths of materialism, cynicism—and irony. (257)

Thompson makes it clear that irony is not a "mere" trope with simply "rhetorical" consequences; its capacity for negation, involving reversal of meaning, is generalized to spiritual malaise and warfare. Having invoked "the last horrible holocaust," he goes on to conclude "that spiritual ironists are sick souls, and that irony as a weapon is usually a method of destruction" (257). It is difficult to imagine the same charges being leveled at a "metaphorist," for example, or a "metonymist."

A more philosophically respectable indictment of the dangers of irony comes from Soren Kierkegaard in *The Concept of Irony*. He distinguishes between two kinds of irony, one directing itself against particular things, and one directing itself against the totality of existence. He argues, like Hegel before him, that this latter kind of irony leads to "infinite absolute negativity": "It is negativity because it only negates; it is infinite because it negates not this or that phenomenon; and it is absolute because it negates by virtue of a higher which is not. Irony establishes nothing, for that which is to be established lies behind it. It is a divine madness which rages like a Tamerlane and leaves not one stone standing upon another in its wake" (278). Because of its nearly supernatural powers of destruction, Kierkegaard argues that it must be "mastered" in a dialectic move beyond mere negativity. Unmastered, irony provides "this eternity void of content, this bliss without enjoyment, this superficial profundity, this hungry satiety" (302).

Such forces of negation can, however, be harnessed for positive ends. Because it depends on a dissimulation—the pretense of saying one thing and meaning another—irony is associated with the general misuse of rhetoric; but because of its self-reflexivity, it is also associated with the critical spirit of self-consciousness, of dialectical inquiry. In its mastered moment, Kierkegaard praises irony's restorative powers, arguing that the person who does not understand irony properly "lacks what at moments is indispensable for the personal life, lacks the bath of regeneration and rejuvenation, the cleansing baptism of irony that redeems the soul . . ." (339). He associates irony with the truth of true dialectic, and claims then that irony is "like the negative way, not the truth but the way" (340). Kierkegaard's argument makes clear why irony (as, of course, we know of other tropes) cannot be seen simply as a static trope, a self-contained figure one employs as a tool. Rather, irony is something that is always viewed *in relation* to that which it negates. It is a process—like thinking, or like revolution.

Kierkegaard's association of irony with dialectic—an association Kenneth Burke later makes as well—is consistent with the valorization of irony as the trope of self-consciousness. Hayden White, for example, argues that in "Irony"

> figurative language folds back upon itself and brings its own potentialities for distorting perception under question. This is why characterizations of the world cast in the Ironic mode are often regarded as *intrinsically* sophisticated and realistic. They appear to signal the ascent of thought in a given area of inquiry to a level of self-consciousness on which a genuinely "enlightened"—that is to say, self-critical—conceptualization of the world and its processes has become possible. (37)

White's tropological view of history is indebted to Vico's use of tropes to characterize historical epochs. "The first men of the gentile world," Vico argues, "were as simple as children, who are truthful by nature"; irony, then, "could certainly have begun only in the age of reflection, for it is formed from falsehood by dint of a reflection which borrows a mask of truth" (225). Irony, then, is a sign of the postlapsarian world, a fall from the age of innocence (and metaphor) into an age of experience and knowledge. Similarly, Walter J. Ong argues that, while the ancient world and oral cultures certainly rely on irony, it is with print culture that irony really takes hold (27). The power associated with irony in the modern age is thus connected with sophisticated literacy.

Historically, the social status of the ironist has undergone many changes. In classical antiquity, the figure of the *eiron* was associated with sly-foxery, and irony was considered somewhat vulgar. Beginning roughly in the Enlightenment period, however, it seems primarily associated with the refined rhetoric of the aristocracy—and its decadence.[1] By the late nineteenth century, it became the voice of such alienated intellectuals as Thomas Hardy and Oscar Wilde. Whatever the status, the ironist makes a pretense at least of superiority. Kierkegaard, for example, notes that there is an exclusiveness about irony, arguing that

> this figure of speech looks down, as it were, on plain and ordinary discourse immediately understood by everyone; it travels in an exclusive incognito ... and looks down from its exalted station with compassion on ordinary pedestrian speech. ... Insofar as the higher circles (naturally this must be understood according to an intellectual protocol) speak ironically—just as kings and rulers speak French so as not to be understood by commoners—to this extent irony is in the process of isolating itself, for it does not generally wish to be understood. (265–66)

By associating irony with the language of "kings and rulers," Kierkegaard suggests that it is a discourse of power. It operates like a special language, excluding those who cannot, according to the rules by which power is conferred, understand or speak it. These latter are, in Kierkegaard's terms, the "commoners." In a later (1906) version of this same idea, George Palante argues—with no apparent irony—that resistance to irony is generally a mark of intellectual simplicity, thereby accounting for its unpopularity not only among commoners, but among women as well.

> The common people see in irony an arrogance of intellect, an insult to Caliban. As for woman, she is like the common people in her lack of understanding and her contempt for the intellect. Schopenhauer's paradox remains true. Woman is above all a physiology and a sensibility, not a mind. To her, irony, a cerebral attitude in which the primacy of the intellect over sensibility is affirmed, is suspicious and antipathetic. (157, translation mine)

Assertions such as Palante's cannot, of course, be read as empirical fact but as evidence of the ideological coding of rhetoric and power.

It is this connection between irony and power that explains, I think, why the cautions against the possible misuses of irony seem to exceed those against other figures (where the stakes are lower) and why, indeed, irony has proved so difficult to control. Irony helps mark the differences between master and mastered—teacher and student, expert and novice writer. Such differences preserve the hierarchies that guarantee reason, meaning, class structure, gender, and power. Whether "kings and rulers" really do speak the language of irony is not, for my present purposes, as important as the fact that irony is *figured* as a figure of power.

Unfortunately, the ability to understand irony may seem an accurate indicator of the difference between teacher and student in the writing classroom. In the classroom setting, lower-division writing students show a remarkable if not alarming inability to detect irony in their reading or to use it in their writing. Yet they are not unfamiliar with the trope; on the contrary, students—and women and the common people, for that matter—speak the language of irony all the time. They use it in talking with each other; they discern it in such popular sources as song lyrics or bumper stickers; and they may even, on occasion, enter their writing class remarking how much they are looking forward to writing that day.

But in the classroom, these same students may well miss other forms of irony, including ones that seem to their teachers fairly obvious. There are at least three reasons for this: first, students may lack sufficient contextual information to interpret an ironic text; second, they may apply a limited or inappropriate set of reading conventions to these texts; and third, they may lack practice at the sorts of critical reading and thinking skills that irony often requires.

As teachers, we may be engaging in practices that promote these very problems.

Here, for an example of an ironic text, is an editorial by Jody Powell. It begins straightforwardly enough:

> One lesson from Beirut is that the Delta Force, that highly trained and motivated team designed to rescue Americans held by terrorists, is of limited utility.
>
> That should be no surprise. The feasibility of any military operation is affected by such external factors as distance, time, adequate intelligence and the like.

These statements seem intended to be taken "literally." The diction is guarded, and the claim is so qualified ("limited utility") that a vague reference to "external factors" serves as support. Military intervention in hostage situations cannot *always* succeed, he suggests, because its success is compromised by such things as "distance, time, adequate intelligence and the like." We might infer that those who think otherwise are thus *not* reasonable.

And, indeed, this is what Powell proceeds to argue:

> However, there are among my colleagues working in the commentating and columnizing business those who argue that the real problem has to do with something more fundamental. As they see it, the real limit on the use of bombs, bullets and other exciting devices is our wimpish obsession with innocent human life. . . . If we would just stop worrying about getting people killed, America could stand tall once again.
>
> Others of my colleagues take a different view. And some, I regret to say, have been excessively harsh and personal in their reactions. A few have gone so far as to charge that these blood-and-gut pundits have never had to accept responsibility for any action more serious than a missed deadline, or that they have never faced anything more violent than a savage book review.
>
> Now that is unfair—even dangerous. If you're going to hold commentators accountable for the consequences of their recommendations, or demand that they know whereof they speak, just go ahead and repeal the First Amendment and be done with it.

The shift to an ironic stance occurs in the first sentence of this passage, but the signals require a shift in the persona of the *reader* that most undergraduates have not learned—and perhaps have not been encouraged—to make *in the classroom*. To perceive, for example, that the word "business" in this context, and especially the adjectival forms of the words "commentators" and "columnists," undercut the persona of the author—set it apart from the real Jody Powell—requires not only an acute sensitivity to style, but also a willingness to see oneself as a superior person, a better user of language, and therefore an ally of Jody Powell against the buffoon who is emerging as the persona in the text. To refer to a bomb as an "exciting device," or to the goal of punishing terrorists without sacrificing lives of innocent hostages as a "wimpish obsession" further separates Powell from the persona he creates—but primarily for those readers who are themselves not obsessed with punishing terrorists, no matter the cost.

To read the passage as irony, we read the sentences *contextually*, recognizing that to label the concern for human life a "wimpish obsession" so overrides cultural conventions about the sanctity of "life" that Powell intends the phrase to be read ironically. To decode the advice to "just go ahead and repeal the First Amendment and be done with it" requires an awareness of what the First Amendment is and an understanding of what Powell, as a columnist, has at stake in the rights of the press. Finally we position ourselves in relation to the tensions Powell has created among himself, his readers, and the preposterous persona in the text. Irony—like all tropes—does not exist so much *in* the text as it does in the relations among multiple voices in the text and in the reader's response to it. It is intersubjective, dialogic (Handwerk 3–4). In this sense, irony demonstrates the need to understand writing as a social practice, as the production and reception of meaning in social and political terms.

In a survey I conducted among approximately 350 students enrolled in an introductory writing course, I found that a majority of students recognized the irony of Powell's editorial and were able to summarize it adequately. Some students were able to provide an analysis of Powell's rhetorical strategies, and some, inspired by the irony in Powell's editorial, used irony in response: "What happens after we eliminate a few groups of terrorists (along with a few groups of our unforgettable newscasters)? Who will we teach to read the teleprompter with the heart, soul, and finesse that these mindless (but lovable) people once did?"

However, a significant minority of the students either do not detect the irony or have difficulty writing about it. Their misunderstanding marks them as part of the audience excluded and makes them, in a certain sense, part of the ironic joke. Here is one example from a student essay:

> In this article Jody Powell is taking a stand against America's reaction to terrorist actions. He is basically stating that the US should be more bold in its decision-making related to terrorism. The statement is made that the United States should sacrifice the lives of our country men in order to uphold our status as proud nation willing to fight for its cause. One might say that this stand on the issue is inhumane and risky. Also who is going to volunteer on such a suicide mission and would it ever bring an end to terrorist actions?

The problem in this student's text is not a matter of grammatical competence, but of *interpretive* competence. This student recognizes that Powell's plan, as stated literally, may seem "inhumane" and "risky"; that is, the student has apparently sensed a conflict between what Powell is proposing and what might seem reasonable. But the student does not try to solve this incongruity by reading Powell's essay as an example of irony, and instead attempts to find coherence in the text, overlooking much evidence that would contradict a literal reading.

Here is another example of a student who misses the irony, and thereby misses the point:

> Although Jody Powell's idea appears to have many hopes, it just does not show any signs of feasibility. At times her idea has some logic to it; however, there are many bugs in it.
>
> Miss Powell would like to SWAP our commentators from our country for hostages held in other countries. With this idea, America could be absolutely free. The idea is spectacular. We would receive coverage from all over the world along with returning our citizens to their homes and loved ones.
>
> As wonderful as this sounds, underlying problems arise. It is difficult to believe that so many commentators would agree to put their lives on the line and at such a high risk. Would they really be as willing as the author assumes?

Again, the student notices the incongruity, but imagines that Powell has not. The confusion over Powell's gender shows more than lack of familiarity with an unusual name; it suggests the absence of the historical and political knowledge that the essay tacitly relies on for its effect.

Students may be unfamiliar both with historical context and with certain interpretive conventions. As work in the area of reader-response has argued, reading irony dramatizes our reliance on a complicated set of expectations and shared social and cultural experience necessary to all reading (see Culler 155). In ordinary conversation, we judge a statement to be ironic according to our shared knowledge of external contexts and our familiarity with the speaker's point of view. In the case of writing, however, our ability to construe a statement or text as being ironic depends on the familiarity with textual conventions of interpretation and *vraisemblance* (Booth, Culler, Fish, Muecke, Suleiman)—and with what is *conventionally* taken to be a plausible model of the human world. Helping students read irony, then, requires that we provide access to the social and rhetorical contexts for the texts we bring to the classroom.

If teaching the reading of irony is a step toward empowering students, ironic writing is the next step. Yet some of the advice we give to students about how to write might suggest that "good" writers do not write ironically; rather, they write clearly, directly, literally. In the examples cited above, for example, students recognized Powell's violation of the conventions of *vraisemblance*, but missed his irony by assuming that he was "sincere" in what he said. And, of course, he was. But the model of clarity and sincerity we teach may lead students to believe there is a conflict between clarity and irony.

The principles of clarity and sincerity underpinning the teaching of writing at the undergraduate level, buttressed by research in readability, encourage a style of writing that attempts to make few demands for interpretation on the reader. John Trimble, for example, tells us that *good writers* assume "that whatever isn't plainly stated the reader will invariably misconstrue. . . . They assume that even their profoundest ideas are capable of being expressed clearly" (Trimble 20). That clarity is not simply a stylistic virtue but a moral one as well is explicit in the opening statement to Joseph Williams' textbook on style: "This is a short book with a simple thesis: it's good to write clearly, and anyone can" (*Style: Ten Lessons in Clarity and Grace* 2). Elsewhere, and perhaps ironically, Williams points out that there may even be an economic argument for clear writing

("Style and Its Consequences" 445–46)—efficiency is a virtue both in writing and in the marketplace.

Irony is not incompatible, of course, with either clarity or grace, and neither Trimble nor Williams says that it is. Nor can one disagree with their advice; *most* of us think it is "good" to be "clear." However, in the majority of our current textbooks, discussions of figurative language in general are entirely absent or greatly reduced—usually to metaphor, simile, and possibly analogy. By largely ignoring figurative language, these textbooks suggest that to be clear, one need also be *literal*. The texts imply that figurative language is something one adds on to make a text more "vivid," though students are advised not to "add" too much. As Frederick Crews warns in *The Random House Handbook*, "Figurative language . . . is as tricky as it is useful. When you intend an abstract meaning, you have to make sure that your dead metaphors stay good and dead. And when you do wish to be figurative, see whether you are getting the necessary vividness and consistency. If not, go back to literal statement; it is better to make plain assertions than to litter your verbal landscape with those strangled hulks" (233). This warning is an example of what Paolo Valesio calls "the rhetoric of antirhetoric" (41), the use of figurative language employed, in this case ironically, to warn against the use of figurative language. The warning is consistent with the conventional view that figurative language is at odds with clarity and therefore must be repressed in the interests of making meaning transparent.

The opposition between plain prose and figurative language also underpins the opposition between nonliterary and literary forms. "One of the conventions of the expository essay," George Dillon points out, "says that figurative language, broadly construed . . . plays a more limited and ancillary role in essays than in some other types of writing. In part, this is so because the expository essay has little use for expressive language generally (e.g., to evoke moods and atmospheres or convey impressions). Further, figurative language is not expected to carry the communicative weight that it does in poetry" (154–55). Thus, while figurative language in general, and irony in specific, have been staples of literary studies, they have been seen as largely irrelevant to the study of nonliterary writing. From the conservative standpoint of the New Critics, for whom irony was the principle of all "good" poetry, to the Marxist orientation of Lukács, for whom irony defined the condition of the novel, irony and literature have been intimately linked. But composition studies has had to struggle with its relationship to "literature" (or, more specifically, literature departments), and this has no doubt exacerbated the tendency in composition to make rather unproblematized distinctions—between, for example, literary and nonliterary writing, expression and communication, imagination and reason. The college essay is not expected to resemble what the great essayists have written; indeed, what we admire in the work of someone like Montaigne is the presence of the very "literary" elements that we discourage in our own students' essays.

There is a disparity, then, between the kind of writing we encourage students to write, and the kind of writing they encounter all around them in the college classroom. The figurative—and ironic—elements are pervasive not only in the genres we teach—various modes of autobiographical writing, expository and persuasive texts—but also in reports and memos, in the news every day, and even on bumper stickers: "One nuclear bomb can ruin your whole day." So why do we not teach irony?

There are some compelling practical answers to this question. The composition course has been saddled with an impossible burden, required already to address such a variety of skills in such a short period of time that there does not seem to be any more room in the curriculum. In this context, it seems reasonable to begin teaching writing as a matter of "saying what you mean" as simply and directly as possible, a sort of preliminary to being able to manipulate language in more complex ways. Given the limitations of time and place, teachers of writing must necessarily make priorities about what they choose to teach. And there is the additional problem that even if one wants to teach irony, few aids exist in this pedagogical area, textbooks being only the most obvious missing component.

Perhaps an unconscious reason for our slighting of irony has to do, as Kierkegaard intuited, with a question of power. Research by Sarah Freedman shows, for example, that while professional writers assume authority in relation to their audience, student writers tend to adopt subordinate roles. In attempting to assess differences in quality between professional and student writers, Freedman found that one of the striking differences—though not necessarily a qualitative one—was that the professional writers used an informal and casual tone, whereas students tended to adopt a formal tone, the "natural" register for classroom writing. She hypothesizes that students, because they lack authority, must "use linguistic forms that show respect, deference, and the proper degree of formality" (341). When we demand clarity and sincerity from student writing—that students say what they mean and mean it—we are asking them to be rhetorically deferent. We are also forbidding them the position of the ironist, who says something *other* than what he or she means, and in doing so, seems to be calling into question the notion, in Grice's terms, that discourse is essentially "cooperative."[2] The ironist, far from being cooperative, seems distant, perhaps recalcitrant (one thinks of Socrates feigning sympathetic interest in pursuing his interlocutor's train of thought), capable even of a little cruelty. Thus, for example, as an expert, Crews has the authority to use the very rhetoric he warns students against. And in his specific warnings against irony, he implies that student writers lack the "light touch" that it takes to handle irony effectively, and he suggests, "Your wisest course . . . may be to pass up chances to write whole essays governed by an ironic stance. Try instead, if you wish, to get occasional effects of irony through understatement" (14). Thomas Whissen issues a similar warning: "A little irony goes a long way. Overused, it can become cloying and make the writer seem smug, waspish, cynical. In the hand of masters like Jonathan Swift or Oscar Wilde it can retain its brilliance and bite, but the rest of us are better off indulging in it sparingly lest it backfire and make us sound 'cute' instead of clever" (75).

That Crews advocates understatement, rather than overstatement, is consistent with the demand that students show deference—and good taste. Overstatement—a sign, perhaps, of excess or copiousness—would then be reserved for those who have earned the right to break—and make—conventions. Apparently, irony is, or should be, as foreign to students as Palante thought it to be to women and the common people. We ask students not to use irony, yet we extol, for wielding their ironic pens, those authors canonized in one anthology after another as models to imitate or contemplate (Forster, Orwell, White, Woolf, etc.). In short, in requiring students to be "literal," we reserve the right to change meaning—to be figurative—to specialists. We reserve the powers of irony for those in power, and teach the equivalent of ironing to our students. In doing so, we risk reproducing the very power structure that informs the situation of writing today, for writing—or the writing instructor at least—has already been relegated to the ironing board.

How might we address the absence of irony in our curriculum? Clearly, it would not suffice simply to include irony among other figures covered in a section on figurative language—although that might be a beginning. We need to pay more attention to the larger issue of texts in their contexts, to see what is at stake in the writing we read and the writing we produce. A curriculum that includes the problem of irony will have to acknowledge the *social* dimension of writing and reading: to make evident the power relations embedded in the acts of reading and writing and to see language not simply as a neutral (clear, sincere) medium, but as an interested one. A focus on these relations implies a focus on whole texts, rather than on extracts, and on texts as they are related to other texts, rather than on texts isolated from their reasons for being written. Teaching irony is more than teaching a trope; it means teaching critical thinking, reading, and writing.

If, as Kierkegaard asserted, irony is the language of "kings and rulers," then there is some irony in the claims prevalent in composition studies that students gain power by writing clear, direct, and, by implication, unironic prose. Of course, irony is not the only language of power, nor by teaching it will we turn all our students into its masters. We can profit, however, by examining what it "means" to "say what we mean." And we have an obligation to enable our students to see the irony of "bombs, bullets and other exciting devices," rather than to remain its witless victims.

Notes

1. See J. A. K. Thompson, *Irony: An Historical Introduction,* for a history of the concept of irony during the classical period.

2. Grice has, however, attempted to reconcile irony with his cooperative principle. See David Holdcroft, "Irony as Trope, and Irony as Discourse."

Works Cited

Booth, Wayne C. "A New Strategy for Establishing a Truly Democratic Criticism." *Daedalus* 112.1 (Winter 1983): 193–214.

———. *A Rhetoric of Irony.* Chicago: U of Chicago P, 1974.

Burke, Kenneth. *A Grammar of Motives.* Berkeley: U of California P, 1969.

Crews, Frederick, and Ann Jessie Van Sant. *The Random House Handbook.* 4th ed. New York: Random, 1984.

Culler, Jonathan. *Structuralist Poetics: Structuralism, Linguistics and the Study of Literature*. Ithaca, NY: Cornell UP, 1975.

Dillon, George. *Constructing Texts: Elements of a Theory of Composition and Style*. Bloomington: Indiana UP, 1981.

Fish, Stanley. "Short People Got No Reason to Live: Reading Irony." *Daedalus* 112.1 (Winter 1983): 175–91.

Freedman, Sarah Warshauer. "The Registers of Student and Professional Expository Writing: Influences on Teachers' Responses." *New Directions in Composition Research*. Ed. Richard Beach and Lillian Bridwell. New York: Guilford, 1984, 334–47.

Handwerk, Gary J. *Irony and Ethics in Narrative: From Schlegel to Lacan*. New Haven: Yale UP, 1986.

Holdcroft, David. "Irony as Trope, and Irony as Discourse." *Poetics Today* 4.3 (1983): 493–512.

Kierkegaard, Soren. *The Concept of Irony*. Trans. Lee M. Capel. Bloomington: Indiana UP, 1965.

Mann, Thomas. *The Magic Mountain*. Trans. H. T. Lowe-Porter. New York: Knopf, 1975.

Muecke, D. C. *The Compass of Irony*. London: Methuen, 1969.

Ohmann, Richard. "Use Definite, Specific, Concrete Language." *College English* 41.6 (Dec. 1979): 390–97.

Ong, Walter J., S.J. "From Mimesis to Irony: The Distancing of Voice." *The Horizon of Literature*. Ed. Paul Hernadi. Lincoln: U of Nebraska P, 1982. 11–42.

Palante, George. "L'ironie: étude psychologique." *Revue philosophique de la France et de l'etranger* 61 (Feb. 1906): 147–63.

Powell, Jody. "Let a *SWAP* Team (Of Know-it-all Pundits) Deal with Terrorists." *Los Angeles Times*, July 5, 1985.

Suleiman, Susan. "Interpreting Ironies." *Diacritics* 6.2 (Summer 1976): 15–21.

Thompson, Alan Reynolds. *The Dry Mock: A Study of Irony in Drama*. Berkeley and Los Angeles: U of California P, 1948; rpt. Philadelphia: Porcupine Press, 1980.

Thompson, J. A. K. *Irony: An Historical Introduction*. London: Allen, 1926.

Trimble, John R. *Writing with Style: Conversations on the art of writing*. Englewood Cliffs, NJ: Prentice, 1975.

Valesio, Paolo. *Novantiqua: Rhetorics as a Contemporary Theory*. Bloomington: Indiana UP, 1980.

Vico, Giambattista. *Selected Writings*. Ed. and trans. Leon Pompa. Cambridge: Cambridge UP, 1982.

Whissen, Thomas. *A Way With Words: A Guide for Writers*. Oxford: Oxford UP, 1982.

White, Hayden. *Metahistory: The Historical Imagination in Nineteenth-Century Europe*. Baltimore: Johns Hopkins UP, 1973.

Williams, Joseph M. *Style: Ten Lessons in Clarity and Grace*. 2nd ed. Glenview, IL: Scott, 1985.

———. "Style and Its Consequences: Do as I Do, Not as I Say." *College English* 43.5 (Sept. 1981), 433–51.

9

What Stands for What: Kenneth Burke on Spirit and Sign

Ellen Quandahl

If students' reading and writing practices mirror a body of teaching practices, then thematics, reading for announced themes or projects, for the central ideas of texts, and a related procedure, symbolics, searching out "key symbols," and using those themes and symbols as the subject of essays, dominate composition pedagogy today. Commercial publishers, continually producing new "readers," collections of essays and stories selected and grouped thematically, both support and are supported by this dominant pedagogy. Trained by teachers and textbooks in thematics, students will insist that *Romeo and Juliet* is a play about star-crossed lovers who are fated to die. They have heard this reading from their teachers, but also rely upon two lines, from two textual authorities, the Chorus and the Prince, who announce this interpretation: "A pair of star-cross'd lovers take their life" (6), and "heaven finds means to kill your joys with love" (5.3.293). Students' writing about the play is frequently an effort to amplify these announcements, and it ignores the metaphorical activity of the text that provides other, even contrary interpretations. Symbolic readers, to use another well-known example, will often write about how, in *The Great Gatsby,* the green light symbolizes hope and new life, and is the key to the text. They rely less upon an interpretation announced by the text than upon connecting a symbol with a system of meanings that is simply "given"—given by

113

the teacher—and that remains unexplored as a system of literary conventions. This method of reading also discourages students from exploring their responses to the text.

Thematic and symbolic readings produce stable meanings and are conducive to compositions with clear theses and arguments. Many students are very good at both procedures, and it is to their credit that they have, no matter what their sentences and spelling look like, learned their lessons so well. When university teachers claim that students' readings are rigid, conservative, and commonplace, they ignore the extent to which pedagogy has ignored the performative aspect of texts, the ways in which language operates to add to, counter, or adjust "central" themes. An alternative pedagogy must not merely correct (e.g., "Act III runs counter to your thesis"; "Is this the *only* reading the text suggests?"), but will need to teach new ways of reading through writing. This is especially important if students are not to feel, upon entering the university, that they must simply swallow a *new* set of themes and symbols (e.g., "*Romeo and Juliet* is a play about a political economy in which a woman will be cast into the streets if she does not marry whom her father wills.").

The work of Kenneth Burke offers an alternative language for pedagogy. But before turning to it, I want to comment on the relation of Burke to rhetoric/composition and to this book. First, it must be acknowledged that there is already a tradition of familiarity, among composition teachers, with Burke as a source of theoretical insight. In numerous conversations I have participated in, about Burkean interpretation or pedagogy, someone has suggested that Burke's is a contextual rhetoric based on drama—that he teaches us how it makes sense to talk about an act of speech or writing only in relation to scene, agency, purpose, and so on. And further, that for any given subject about which one may wish to write, to *name* the five elements (Burke's "pentad") of that subject's drama is the beginning of invention. Another variation of this conversation is that the writer (agent) must understand the scene (audience, time, and place) in which he or she is writing. And certainly Burke, who knows his Aristotle, does remind us that it is easier to praise Athens among the Athenians than among the Spartans. In other words, it is possible to identify *topoi* of Burkean pedagogy, and also to revise them.

Second, in recent years there has been, in the rhetoric and composition journals, a prolific rush to affiliate Burke with new theory. In a handful of articles, one finds his name linked with all of the following: Barthes, Kuhn, Gramsci, Hugh Kenner, Freud, Iser, Perlman, Marx, Derrida, modernism, postmodernism, pluralism, psychoanalysis, and "Heidegger's French descendants" (Warnock 67). In part, these affiliations are a healthy move away from using the few systematic elements in the Burke corpus as heuristics for writing and toward a more "philosophic" discussion of Burke as reader. But I suspect that they are partly a defensive move, too, claiming that the Burke we have known for years both precedes and supersedes what the fancy critics are doing in language that, for all its authority, is impossibly abstract.

My aim in this essay, given these contexts, becomes threefold: to explore and plunder Burke's texts for pedagogy, to offer an alternative or revisionary representation of Burke's contextual rhetoric, and to illustrate how, as a reader of textual activity, Burke both belongs in this volume and is different from other theorists represented here. To say that Burke is a poststructuralist, or an early deconstructionist—now familiar claims—simply will not do. With all three of these contexts in mind, I will explore one strand of Burke's philosophy, the well-known idea that words are (symbolic) action. I will show, in contrast to the view of language contained in thematics and symbolics, that meanings are active and unstable because they abbreviate highly complex contexts—the view contained in Burke's idea that "words inspirit things." And finally, I will sketch a pedagogy designed to teach the power of words to metamorphose things as they "carry contexts" to them.

Signs/Spirit/Metaphor

In 1956 Burke gave a talk at the Human Relations Center at Boston University, at which speakers were invited to reverse a commonly held notion. The talk, published in *Anthropological Linguistics* as "What Are the Signs of What?" reversed the idea that words are the signs of things and argued that things are the signs of words, indeed that things are "inspirited" by words, that words communicate "spirit" to things.[1] Without recommending it as a theology, Burke finds the metaphorical concept of inspiriting much to his purpose in analyzing language. The reversal, as Burke notes, is a variant of Emerson's claim that natural facts are signs of spiritual facts, and it doubles back on an idea to which Burke has returned repeatedly over the years, that whatever you can say about God in the theological realm, you can say about language in the logological (words about words).[2] The essay promises to talk about signs and referents, something we might expect to understand in contradistinction to a post-Saussurean framework, which has so little to say about "real" referents, and everything to say about signifieds. But Burke's argument finally works against the comparison, for about midway we read that, "Regrettably" the view of language as action "does not spontaneously favor a theory of signs" (367) at all. In the revision of the essay for the University of California Press edition of 1966, Burke renames his problematic not as the distorting relationship of signs to things (as in the first published version) but as "radically involved with variations on Spinoza's concept of substance (as overall situational context)" (360). It is this problematic I want to explore, in order to offer a revision of Burke as contextualist.

Much of the essay centers on explaining the way in which words exist in and abbreviate complex nonverbal situations. While Burke suggests that we perceive the world through language,[3] he does not make the Derridean move to say that all is text, but rather explores the idea that contexts are the "nonverbal, or less-than-verbal, or more-than-verbal ground" of language (373). Burke preserves, for example, a difference between referents of words about nature and words about sociopolitics. The latter, "with the personal and social relations involved in them, and the vast terminology of attitudes, acts, and motives that goes with them, do not enjoy exactly the kind of extraverbal reality we find in the . . . natural realm; yet they are not identical with the verbal order as such" (375). Still, whether they are about nature, the sociopolitical, the supernatural, or about words themselves, words are "equally real so far as their nature as sheer words is concerned" (374). The nature of words about the supernatural (whatever that might be "in reality") is to inspirit it, to name the supernatural with terms from other contexts. For example, God as father or lord is an inspiriting of the supernatural with the sociopolitical. Nature is similarly inspirited by "a vast network of verbally perfected meanings" derived from people's "cooperative acts" in sociopolitical orders (378). That is, words, by virtue of being of a different order of "reality" than the contexts they summarize, name those contexts inadequately, or overadequately, filling them, as we will see, with attitudes and social ratings. Let us look for a moment at this post-Spinozist concern with "overall situational context."

As we know from the *Grammar,* Burke notices how, grammatically—that is, in texts, in the working out of arguments in texts that pursue the implications of their terms thoroughly—terms are usually grounded in, defined by, what they are not. The most highly generalized example is the philosophical idea that the ground of being is not-being. This "paradox of substance," that a thing's essence or substance is stated in terms of what the thing is not, what stands under it, is the fiction that Derridean philosophy undermines, and the citable textual reality that Burke most frequently pursues. Indeed, the best-known argument from the *Grammar* is that each philosophical school grounds or "substantiates" its arguments in a particular substance-term—materialism substantiating its claims with reference to scene, idealism to agent, and so on.

Now, for Burke, Spinoza is the scenic philosopher *par excellence:*

> Thinking contextually, Spinoza held that each single object in the universe is "defined" (determined, limited, bounded) by the other things that surround it. And in calling upon men to see things "in terms of eternity" (*sub specie aeternitatis*) Spinoza meant precisely that we should consider each thing in terms of its total context, the universal scene as a whole. (*Grammar* 25)

Thus, in the conversation that spurred the publication of "Signs," Burke referred to a tribesman who had one name for a raccoon in one situation, and another name for the animal in a different situation, as "an excellent Spinozist" (360).[4]

In considering the relationship of words to things, Burke follows the Spinozist lead and looks to the relationship of verbal expressions to those complex situations—contexts—which they seem to sum up. His primary illustration is the sentence "The man walks down the street":

> To realize that it is more like the "title" of a situation than like the description of an act, we need but realize that the sentence, as stated, could not be illustrated. For you'd have to picture a tall man, or a short man, a dark man or a light man, etc. He'd have to be pictured as walking upright or bent over, with or without a hat, or a cane, etc. And the street would have to be wide or narrow, with a certain kind of curbing, paving, and the like. It is in this sense that the sentence is to be viewed after the analogy of a title, which sums up an essence or trend or slant, rather than describing the conditions that would be required for the thing named really to happen or exist. (361)

Burke is playing with Berkeley's notion of abstraction, and adds that the summarizing sentence could be further abbreviated, or raised to another order of abstraction, by "street-situation," or even just "street" (371).

Words therefore function synecdochally, but in a complex way (which readers of Freud will recognize as a variant of condensation and displacement). For even as they entitle situations, words summarize secret or repressed situational contexts, as when the term *dog* evokes feelings associated with one's " 'primal' dog, the first dog [one] knew, or loved, or [was] frightened by, or lost" (359; *Action* 73). Moreover, words abbreviate situations yet to evolve, in the sense that they anticipate or gesture toward or imply responses to them (*Grammar* 236–37); words even organize opposition, "counter-assertions," that "come running from all directions, like outlaws in the antique woods converging upon the place where a horn has sounded" (367). And still further, words summarize "social ratings due to the fact that language is a social product, and thus builds the tribe's attitudes into its 'entitlings' and into their 'abbreviations' " (361). From this last example, and in a first pass at the promised reversal, Burke concludes, "Thereby, the things of the world become material exemplars of the values which the tribal idiom has placed upon them" (361).

But in a later, longer version of the reversal-argument, Burke adds another step: things themselves have a summarizing function. A piece of a garment could summarize (synecdochally) the garment, and also (metonymically) the person who has worn it or a similar garment, and even responses to that person (372–73). A post-Saussurean, Barthes, for example, might notice that Burke has in effect demonstrated that things themselves are signifiers and must be considered in a theory of signs and socially imbricated meanings. But Burke's text presses on to consider the relatedness of things and signs, and suggests that once you get to a summarizing word and summarizing object you could say you have "a state of affairs wherein the word is the sign of the thing" (372). A few lines later, however, he suggests that "you have a condition wherein the thing can be taken as the visible manifestation of . . . the corresponding word" (373). Thus, the essay does not fully make good its claim to replace "words stand for things" with "things stand for words"; rather, it illustrates the reversibility of the trope. But what it insists upon is the metaphor of "inspiriting" to describe the relation of verbal to nonverbal synecdoches: just as Emerson's nature manifests—is a sign of—the spirit that pervades it, things are the signs of words because they are inspirited by them. The synecdochic garment, for example, takes on the "spirit"—the emotional intensity, the perspective, the motive—of words attributed to its wearer, and is a sign of them. Words are summarizing containers that transport (carry over, metaphor) to things (which are their context) summaries of other things (which are the contexts of those summaries). Language is fundamentally metaphorical and mediating, a go-between or communicator—between contexts and things and between motives and actions. Burke suggests that this mediating function is a linguistic analogue for the Holy Spirit, the communion between Father (thing named) and Son (name, "the Word") (377–78; *Religion* 29–33).

This last is decidedly not Spinoza, but it picks up on a phrase from Spinoza that Burke mentions so frequently that it becomes a leitmotiv in his philosophy. The phrase is *Deus sive natura,* which Burke translates "God equals Nature," and paraphrases as "action equals motion" (*Grammar* 137). One of the difficulties with Burke's leitmotiv is that he often abbreviates it, using his own "action=motion" to summarize a larger argument. As I understand him, Burke reads Spinoza through Aquinas, Kant, and even William James, to suggest that "we could get God as a scenic word for action" or translate God "as an 'action' word" (*Grammar* 138). That is, there are echoes here of philosophies of God as the ultimate ground of possibility, God as the ultimate act (*causa sui,* unmoved mover), whose creating word is the most complete act, the prototype of all acts (*Grammar* 61, 68). Nature, on the other hand, is merely motion, a structure of events.

For Burke, Spinoza's "equating" of these nonidentical terms is a pivotal argument; the equation allows him to understand early texts—which are replete with God-language—and later texts—which represent the structure of the world without reference to a creator—as functionally related. Burke's discussion of the phrase *Deus sive natura* typifies one of his reading strategies, and it looks like a kind of philosophical history. In such a history, Spinoza's phrase, rendered by Burke as God=Act, becomes a watershed moment in the movement of thought toward "naturalism," the use of nature—a structure or "concatenation of events"—rather than creation—or events enacted (by God)—as the context for understanding (*Grammar* 138). That is, once you have equated nature with God, you can begin to look at the order of nature "efficiently," without considering it as a function of God's ordering act. Reading with this trope in mind, one might say that Thales' belief that "all things are full of gods" (*Grammar* 118) and Foucault's notion that "Power is everywhere" (*History* 93) are statements at the extremes of this watershed, both describing overall situational context. Indeed, Foucault's language about power as "a moving substrate," "constantly *engender(ing)*," "a complex strategical *situation*" (*History* 93, my italics), bears, albeit with a different emphasis, something of the scene-act-God-nature "cluster" Burke reads in Spinoza's equation. Burke might suggest, for example, that the enacting function of God as ultimate—or substantiating—scene persists in Foucault's language about power, although the terms have moved on.

I use this example to illustrate my understanding of a way in which Burke reads (a way I will recommend in the final section, on pedagogy), but also to suggest an ontological notion that seems to intrigue him as a way of explaining context in the broadest sense. It is the notion, emphasized differently by Thales and Foucault, that things are "*powers* or *acts* (acts potentially or actually)," "that in everything there is a power, or motive, of some sort." As Plato suggested in the *Sophist*, "Being [is] 'that which has the power to act or be acted upon'" (*Grammar* 118–20). Burke has a way of resetting philosophical gems like this, so we should consider it in view of his larger project.

As a rhetorician, Burke is always considering arguments and ways of thinking about our socialness. He unfailingly attends to cooperative acts, inducements to and accounts of social behaviors. It is the *social* self, rather than the social *self*—to use one of his favorite tropes—that most engages Burke. He is intrigued by what motivates us to social activity. To understand what moves us is a traditional rhetorical concern. Burke's philosophy dramatically expands that concern, suggesting that to understand motives is to understand that all things are powers. That is, things act, carrying their natures to new contexts metaphorically, or are acted upon and transformed synecdochally. In this way, powers—primal dogs and outlaws in antique woods—can move us. Our acts, therefore, are *symbolic* acts—partial, tendentious, motivated—themselves standing for (symbolizing, metaphorizing) those forces by which we are, in effect, spoken.[5] To name those forces *gods* is much the same as to name them *motives*. For example, Burke says that *driven by the Furies* and *guilt* refer to one condition (*Grammar* 265; 298). And, not surprisingly, he suggests that *motives* are shorthand terms for *situations* (*Permanence* 31).

But Burke also adds to ideas about how we are moved a rather unfashionable (at the moment) element of Cartesianism by looking at *symbolic* acts as symbolic *acts*. He suggests that to study the term "act" thoroughly we need a prototype, which, as we have already seen, is "God's act," God's creating word. Following James, Burke sees God's acts as pure, utterly novel, even magic. (If they were anything less, "God" would not be "God"—unmoved—but motivated.) Similarly, "magic, in the sense of novelty, is seen to exist normally, in some degree, as an ingredient of every human act; for each act contains some measure of motivation that cannot be explained simply in terms of the past, being to an extent, however tiny, a *new thing*" (*Grammar* 65).[6]

In Burke's view, therefore, we are less thoroughly scripted than in, say, Barthes' or Derrida's. In his much-cited definition, we are bodies in action (purposive motion), bodies with minds, bodies that learn language. Burke sees, both in this *topos* and in Spinoza, a "variant of the Cartesian split," which favors mind and the terms related to mind—God/action (366). The terms of Spinoza's equation are not finally equal; rather, God is first among equals, *primus inter pares* (*Grammar* 149). Thus, for Burke (and for Burke's Spinoza), nature is less-than-verbal, and the verbal, verbal action, is supernatural. As God's word of grace is said to perfect nature, so verbal action "perfects" (adds to, explains, and, in its social function, ideologizes) the world (*Religion* 16).

In discussions of how to locate Burke in relation to new theory, then, some people will always come forward to say that some "essentialism" or "humanism" lurks in the texts, that in viewing language as action, Burke pursues the very "spirit" that, say, Derrida shows to be the fictional "outside" of the play of signifiers. And they will be right. But the important use of the metaphors *spirit, grace, communion,* it seems to me, is in showing the way in which, at last, words refuse fixed referents, since they carry abbreviations of present, past, and even future contexts with them. The "Dramatist" approach, the text of the "Signs" essay admits, does not favor a theory of signs, but begins with problems of "transubstantiation" or "transformation"— as when Thales' gods yield to Foucault's power, which takes over their function—or, to use Burke's words, "as when a major term is found somehow to have moved on, and thus to have in effect changed its nature either by adding new meanings to its old nature, or by yielding place to some other term that henceforth takes over its functions wholly or in part" (367). To follow the Spinozistic thread in Burke's philosphy, to say that it is a contextual rhetoric based on drama, then, means that powers are everywhere, inspiriting people, things, words; substantiating and transubstantiating arguments and ways of thinking. In fact, much of Burke's work examines orders of power (eros, knowledge, authority, for example), and ways in which they are often at odds with one another, even within the individual.

Following Burke's pattern of reading rather literally, we see that a contextual rhetoric is not only a matter of naming things in the worlds about which we will speak as scenes or agencies, and so forth. Rather, we read contextually by observing patterns of terms in and among texts, engaging in interpretation and frequently revealing the ideological motives lurking in terms which seem to cover them over. To read like Burke is to read the ways in which terms move on, as new meanings charge, animate, enliven—inspirit—their old natures, or as new words take over those old natures. This same method works for patterns of transformation between texts (Thales to Foucault); or within a single text (*Deus sive natura*), inspirited as it is by other texts, and establishing, as it surely does, equivalences, "whereby terms are treated as overlapping in their jurisdiction, and . . . even sometimes identical" (369).

Pedagogical Summary

Having gone, as Burke would say, rather far afield from the pedagogical issues with which I began this essay, I want now to summarize the theoretical material, recalling that summaries will use parts to refer to the whole, stressing those parts at the expense of others, and that the contexts with which I am working will give them a particular slant. I will take up the three contexts in reverse order, to end where I began, and to give full emphasis to pedagogy.

The Spinozist strand of Burke's philosophy and its tie-ups with metaphysics and theology distinguish Burke sharply from those called poststructuralists. That is, the discourses that sound in Burke are not, for example, the post-Saussurean, or -Peircean, or -Lévi-Straussean. While Burke's discussion of meanings yielding to later texts and changing contexts seems close to Peirce's "commutability" of signifieds or to Derrida's "supplementarity," Burke comes at his version of the idea through another set of terms and references, another history. We need to study these terms in *their* specificity, to observe their performance, to "read" theory just as we "read" "literature" and our students' texts. Critical theories are acts, and we need detailed analyses of their differences as well as their thematic similarities, especially if we are reading to find—not to overlook—pedagogical "motives." Affiliations are beside the point.

The Burke who writes about "overall situational context" describes context as something very volatile, unstable—the alembic of transformability that many readers will know from the *Grammar*. In addition to, for example, "timely topics" or the body of information about audiences that speakers and writers rely on to gain advantage (one of his definitions of rhetoric), Burke recognizes that "Nature is so 'full of gods' (powers) that a systematic directing of the attention anywhere is quite likely to disclose a new one, some genius local to the particular subject matter" (*Rhetoric* 63). To study how texts, as actions inducing actions and attitudes, shape and are shaped by structures of powers is also rhetoric. Such a study would be diminished by attention only to thematics and symbolics, neglectful of ways in which *terms move on*.

Burke's readings rely on a metaphysical language in which each thing (including each word) is a power. As we have seen, a word or thing acts metaphorically, carrying its nature to new contexts, or is acted upon, entitled, or summarized synecdochally, in ways that give it a particular slant or trend or even transform it utterly. To state the case sparely, the strategic move we see in Burke's contextual readings is this: he notices *what stands for what* or *what equals what*. Across texts, he will look at the point at which a term takes on the flavor, or tone, or function of quite a different term in another text. There is our Thales-Foucault example, and others more powerful—as when Burke shows in Marx's term "conditions," a range of meanings, not merely material or operational (as announced), but also ethical and idealistic, preserving something of Hegel (*Grammar* 204–14). Within a single text, Burke will also notice what equals what. Readers familiar with Burke will recall, for example, his interpretation of *Samson Agonistes,* which begins with the implicit equating of Israelites with the Puritan faction, and notices *what difference* the transformation of "political controversy to high theologic terms" makes—that it is a sort of magnification, sanctioning the poet's own resistance, and suggesting "that a blind Biblical hero *did* conquer," and "that he in his blindness *will* conquer" (*Rhetoric* 5). These two moves—to ask *What equals what?* within and across texts, and a concomitant *What difference does the equation make?* could be used straightforwardly as an alternative to thematic and symbolic reading and composing. Briefly, a course might look like this:

In the selection of texts, we could look to Burke's rhetorical interest in accounts of socialness. (I hear the thematic ring of that statement, and the opposition that may come running. But Burke, perhaps more than any rhetorician to date, speaks to the ancient question of the content of rhetoric. That is the subject of another essay.) A range of texts like Jane Addams' "Utilization of Women in City Government" and "If Men Were Seeking the Franchise," Freud's *Civilization and*

Its Discontents, Burke's "Revolutionary Symbolism in America," and Elder's *Ceremonies in Dark Old Men,* in addition to the texts students write, would provide enough material for a semester's work. (A second problem with "readers" is that they offer more material than one would ever need in a sophisticated writing course, the point of which is not "coverage.") Writing assignments would be designed less to explore the *point* of these texts than their *operations,* in order to develop some critical language for use in reading these and students' own texts. For each reading, students would write at least twice, in response to variations on the questions *What equals what?* and *What difference,* in terms of what we can say about language, *does the equation make?* (Burke's readings favor Hegelian triads, but the course may need to revise that movement, since one of its purposes is to counter the tendency to closure of thematics and symbolics.)

Students would write first about a single text, say *Civilization,* a text appropriate to the course because it does not announce a clear thesis—that is, it resists thematic reading and requires another approach—and because it is replete with transforming metaphors, the narratives Freud constructs about changes and redistributions of libidinal energy. A first assignment could ask students to find and describe places in the text where Freud establishes identities or equations by placing one term in connection with another, so that the terms overlap or refer to similar functions, events, or concepts. Prior to writing, discussion of sections the students find compelling or disconcerting will provide examples: Jesus Christ is a version of the primal father who met death by violence; men's control of fire is the equivalent of controlling their desire to put it out with a stream of urine in homosexual competitions; guilt is the inclination to aggression turned inward. A second paper could get at students' responses to these equations or narrative transformations by offering a theoretical question: What ideas that you have about civilization, about human communities and the ways in which people regulate them, *change* when you use the perspectives (the *this is that*s) of the first paper? Burke has called perspective another name for metaphor (*Grammar* 503–6), and this question really gets at a metalinguistic issue—the relatedness of metaphor (the equivalences) to metamorphosis (the trope on which Freud relies as he develops his notion of civilization as achievements resulting from renounced instinct). But it also provides a way in which students may address their own confrontations with the text, one that allows them to see Freud's perspective *as* perspective, as metaphor different from the metaphors they typically use to describe human achievements and happiness. Therefore, in discussions of students' papers, it will be important to ask the equation question of students' own understandings of, their own writing about, *what is* (what it is that Freud's metaphors have metamorphosed).

Now consider the dyadic approach across texts. Having read *Civilization* and then *Ceremonies*, students could write about the relationship of Mr. Parker to his two sons, and of Theo and Bobby to one another, and about the role of fathers and brothers in *Civilization* (or—for there are many possibilities, once reading is decentered—about the relation of Elder's characters to work, and about the function of work in Freud. And these questions may also be framed as a matter of finding identities: What terms does Freud associate with work?; What *is* work?). A second paper would ask students to consider whether Freud's family members and co-workers function in ways dramatized by the play, although the terms have "moved on." These assignments provide material for discussing interpretation as located in a point of view or perspective. And perspective is not simply a framework for analysis, something "given," but rather something constructed through incongruous (metaphorical) language; it is a way of explaining conduct or motives by the favored terms of a social code (*Permanence* 23).

Finally, having read "Revolutionary Symbolism in America" and "Utilization of Women in City Government," students could first address Addams by asking once again what equals what. For this apparently straightforward text, this could be a matter of list-making: what is what under the proposed heading of government as housekeeping, and what is what under the present heading of government as self-defense. In a second essay, students could explore which terms in Addams have the hortatory function, the appeal of identification, that Burke describes in his analyses of myth and the language of the American Communist party in "Revolutionary Symbolism." This assignment also offers a way for students to *frame* a response to Addams' feminist angle (rather than merely to label it as "great!" or "B.S!"), and to begin to understand ways in which rhetorical "motives" elicit responses. As Burke suggests, a perspective or way of explaining is also "an attempt at socialization," and therefore a matter of "*appeal*" (*Permanence* 24–25).

These are examples of a course about metaphor, about the power of metaphor to go unrecognized in everyday speech, to establish a thing's reality, to persuade by incongruity—"the 'carrying-over' of a term from one realm to another" (*Grammar* 504). It is designed to circumvent the language of "key symbols" (or metaphors or images), and "central themes" that shuts down investigation of texts and leads to premature closure. The course works toward the Aristotelian and Burkean idea of rhetoric as persuasion (including analyses of ways in which students themselves respond to texts), prepared for by assignments about the transforming act, or power, of words to establish identities, in contexts both narrow and broad. It is a rhetoric of reading, in which students read the texts they write just as they read the texts they write about, and in which all of these readings form an "overall situational context."

Notes

1. A revised version was published later in *Language as Symbolic Action* by the University of California Press in 1966. Citations will refer to the California version unless noted by AL—for *Anthropological Linguistics*—in the parenthetical reference. And all parenthetical citations refer to this essay unless noted by other, abbreviated titles. *A Grammar of Motives* will be cited as *Grammar, A Rhetoric of Motives* as *Rhetoric,* and *The Rhetoric of Religion* as *Religion.*

2. For example, this is the basic premise of Burke's *The Rhetoric of Religion.* See especially, "Introduction: On *Theology* and *Logology*" 1–5.

3. The introductory section of the AL version stresses the idea of perceiving through language more heavily than the California version. See also Burke's "Terministic Screens," which amplifies the notion.

4. Dell Hymes tells the story of Burke's comment on the Spinozist raccoon in the introduction to the AL version, p. 4.

5. Burke offers this useful definition of action, which he distinguishes from the motions of our sheerly physical organism: "Action . . . would involve modes of behavior made possible by the acquiring of a conventional, arbitrary symbol system, a definition that would apply to modes of symbolicity as different as primitive speech, styles of music, painting, sculpture, dance, highly developed mathematical nomenclatures, traffic signals, road maps, or mere dreams . . ." ("Motion" 809).

6. Burke considers as an example the act of writing, an act which "brings up problems and discoveries" which (in addition to those that are otherwise motivated) derive from the act itself (*Grammar* 67).

Works Cited

Addams, Jane. "If Men Were Seeking the Franchise." *Jane Addams: A Centennial Reader*. Ed. Emily Cooper Johnson. New York: Macmillan, 1960. 107–13.

———. "Utilization of Women in City Government." *Centennial Reader*. 113–23.

Burke, Kenneth. *A Grammar of Motives*. Berkeley: U of California P, 1974.

———. *Language as Symbolic Action*. Berkeley: U of California P, 1966.

———. "(Nonsymbolic) Motion/(Symbolic) Action." *Critical Inquiry* 4.4 (1978): 809–38.

———. *Permanence and Change*. Berkeley: U of California P, 1987.

———. "Revolutionary Symbolism in America." *American Writers' Congress*. Ed. Henry Hart. New York: International Publishers, 1935. 87–94.

———. *A Rhetoric of Motives*. Berkeley: U of California P, 1969.

———. *The Rhetoric of Religion*. Berkeley: U of California P, 1970.

———. "Terministic Screens." *Symbolic Action* 44–62.

———. "What Are the Signs of What?" *Anthropological Linguistics* 4.6 (1962): 1–23.

Elder, Lonne. *Ceremonies in Dark Old Men*. New York: Farrar, 1969.

Foucault, Michel. *The History of Sexuality*. Vol. 1: *An Introduction*. New York: Random, Vintage, 1980.

Freud, Sigmund. *Civilization and Its Discontents*. Tr. James Strachey. New York: Norton, 1961.

Shakespeare, William. *Romeo and Juliet*. *The Riverside Shakespeare*. Boston: Houghton, 1974.

Warnock, Tilly. "Reading Kenneth Burke: Ways In, Ways out, Ways Roundabout." *College English* 48.1 (Jan. 1986): 62–75.

10

Deconstruction, Process, Writing

Randall Knoper

While some excitement—of both threat and possibility—posed by the entry of poststructuralism into composition theory may still linger in the hopes and fears of our profession, a variety of efforts at unfolding and surveying the pertinence of deconstruction to the teaching of writing have by now made the specter familiar. Proposals for daily use of deconstruction in the classroom now exist, as do more general considerations of the benefits and unhappinesses held in store by the meeting of deconstruction and writing pedagogy. Indeed, enough of these exist to warrant some assessment of the encounter between Derridean thinking and theories about writing and its teaching. Since deconstruction presents itself as a precipitator of change in metaphysics, epistemology, and reason itself, as well as a radically subversive political force, one might expect to see, with this embracing of deconstruction, a correspondingly profound shaking of the foundations in our teaching of writing. But such a shaking is not on the horizon of what still looks like an eminently reasonable and politically unexceptional composition pedagogy. Since profound differences are not there to trace, the task here will instead be to disentangle the interweavings of deconstruction and composition theory in order to point out some of the effects of this meeting, to trace some ways in which deconstruction has been tucked into familiar writing theories and teaching orthodoxies, and to identify loose ends, which if pulled, might yet transform (for better or for worse?) our teaching practices, the institutions these practices support, and most especially, our students' writing.

As a beginning, I would like to mention a brief piece by Denis Donoghue titled "Relax, It's Only a Theory," published in the *New York Times Book Review*. In it, Donoghue tells his readers not to fret about deconstruction. It is only a theory, not a belief—that is, he writes, not a basis for action. It is a seminar topic, a philosophy of the theoretical classroom not a philosophy of the streets, and "nobody proposes to act or to speak according to deconstruction once the seminar is over." Donoghue breaths a sigh of relief that deconstruction has not affected what people do—how they act, how they speak, how they write. His essay, of course, comes in the wake of other versions of this point of view—that, for example, poststructuralist theory is an elitist literary discourse that cannot be translated into individual teaching practices or radical political agency—a suitable matter, in short, for abstract and secluded academic meditation, but otherwise useless. I would like to put these conclusions once again as questions, with special reference to that site of *praxis* and its preparation, the writing classroom. Has deconstruction proved useless for practical affairs in the writing classroom? Has it, can it, or should it affect the way we teach writing, or the kind of writing we teach? If so, why? If not, why not?

For a quick gauge of its effects, let us look for a moment at the comments of an exemplary deconstructionist. If we take J. Hillis Miller's two essays on deconstruction and the teaching of writing ("Composition and Deconstruction" and "The Two Rhetorics") as indices, deconstruction has not and will not alter very much what we do in the composition classroom or the kind of writing we teach there. Miller hints in both essays that there could be a practical—and threatening—effect: deconstruction ought to *kill* composition; an awareness of the disruptive powers of language should prevent compositional control. But he shifts his ground from this disturbing contest between deconstruction and composition to that between reading and writing. There he finds a reconciliation; as his familiar remark has it, "reading is itself a kind of writing, or writing is a trope for the act of reading" ("Composition" 41). From this connection between reading and writing as analogous acts or processes of interpretation (a connection we might all acknowledge), Miller slides into the declaration that deconstructive reading—a kind of tropological analysis he calls "good reading as such"—naturally serves an equally ahistorical standard of "good writing." In other words, the murder of composition by deconstruction is here forestalled as the two are raised up into an ideal of "good" reading and writing, a unity that has always existed and will continue.

Miller, of course, has self-confessed conservative instincts ("Rhetorical Study" 12), and he is the familiar bête noire for those who would save deconstruction from a textual aestheticism and use it as a means of change. But I would like to consider whether his discursive maneuvers might not dramatize and heighten more widespread habits of thought about deconstruction and the teaching of writing, habits characteristic even of the well-meant and sympathetic efforts of those who would use deconstruction to transform writing instruction. Specifically, in the existing efforts to bring deconstruction into the writing classroom, do we not persistently present it as a method of *reading* that leaves intact what we must suppose is the usual outcome of this activity: writing as composition, resolution, retying—"good" writing as textbooks imagine it? Or, in a related move, do we not ally deconstruction with a process pedagogy that relegates deconstructive activity to moments of invention, moments that leave few traces, if any, in the product (where Denis Donoghue could see and worry about them)?

Reasoning that the New Criticism made a powerful alliance with a writing pedagogy (of the so-called current-traditional model) that focused on composition as product, composition theorists friendly to poststructuralism have tried to forge a new alliance between deconstruction and "process pedagogy," an alliance that could displace the previous regime (see Winterowd 79–81; Crowley, "Gorgias" 279; White 188). But using process as the hinge to ally deconstruction with composition asks for some scrutiny, especially because this move defines a version of deconstruction that finally seems to have very little effect on student prose. For example, Edward M. White, in a pioneering 1984 essay tracing and advocating alignments between literary theory and composition pedagogy, writes that poststructuralist theory has understandably found its way into our thinking about writing because its version of reading as a meaning-making process suits theories of writing as process (189).

While this assertion should quickly gain assent, White's story of this correspondence and commerce foregrounds the problems I have mentioned. First, like Miller, he identifies poststructuralism as a theory of reading, not of writing; this move rests on the opposition between reading as analysis and writing as composition, and it effectively keeps deconstruction at one remove from the writerly act. Second, he links deconstruction to "writing as process" in a way that conceives "process" as activities of invention and revision that take place before the writing is unveiled for the reader's eyes, or at least that occur someplace other than the presented page, which only inadvertently might betray symptoms of poststructuralist activity. In the familiar phrase, his attention is not on *what* the student writes, but on *how* the student writes; his concern, he claims, lies especially with "the flux of ideas behind the writing," where invention, revision, and deconstruction meet and mingle (191).

This view retains a notion of a "product" created and supported by that backstage sector of chaotic process and messy meaning that, like a contractor's litter, is cleaned up and hidden before the final, balanced, centered edifice is presented to view. We need not be surprised at this, since process pedagogy in most of its forms chose not to challenge essays well made into hierarchical structures—with theses and clear directions, cues, and prescriptions for reading; it simply asserted that we should teach the activity of this making, not only the result. What a student writer would finally let go of—thanks to plenty of playful and rigorous activity in invention and revision—could be formally and stylistically similar to what was produced under the regime of product-oriented pedagogy.

White has been joined by many others; a review of the existing essays on deconstruction and composition shows that most of them tend to veer away from the implications deconstruction has for concrete student texts, for "products," by invoking "process" and then tucking deconstruction away in backstage activities of reading (rather than writing), invention, and revision. In one of the more compelling essays on deconstruction and the teaching of writing, for example, David Kaufer and Gary Waller immediately echo J. Hillis Miller. Titled "To Write Is to Read Is to Write, Right?" the essay cogently translates deconstruction into a pedagogy that stresses reading and writing as perpetual processes of the reconstruction, rearrangement, exploration, and testing of knowledge. While such teaching would plausibly make some difference in student writing— by encouraging students to conceive of a text as a structure of inclusions and exclusions, to understand that the perspectives one brings to a text will shape what one finds, to write their texts as momentary entries in an ever-changing conversation—here the main difference finally appears to be in reading, in what students write about (the content), or in what they do while they do it, not in the compositions they end up with. For when the authors turn specifically to teaching writing, they distill their poststructuralist pedagogy down to some lessons writing teachers would find familiar: teach the activity of problem analysis in a way undifferentiated from Linda Flower and Young, Becker, and Pike; help students grasp knowledge as conflicted, in contest—but mainly as conceptual support for the standard exhortation to consider your opponent; promote the understanding of style and grammar as contextual. All of these are worthy lessons to help students compose and persuade, and the authors lucidly show how deconstruction can be enlisted to undergird them. But if deconstruction is presented as a support for composing practices we already teach, and for a familiar model of good prose, where is the difference?

The most common tendency in the current thinking about poststructuralism and the teaching of writing is to equate deconstruction with invention. For example, according to one essay in the collection edited by C. Douglas Atkins and Michael L. Johnson, *Writing and Reading Differently: Deconstruction and the Teaching of Composition and Literature,* deconstruction belongs in an "inspiration" stage of writing, a "rehearsal-for-writing" stage, where its capacity to aid invention will "improve" the final product by enabling fresh insights into the object of study. Deconstruction becomes here a step in a natural process that dispels in the end the uncertainty deconstruction fosters in "prewriting" (Northam 115–28). In joining deconstruction to process, William Covino also links it to invention, arguing that invention *is* a "process of finding differences [in Derrida's sense]" (1), and conversely, that *différance* ("a process rather than a product" [3]) is unquestionably a matter of invention. Gregory L. Ulmer makes his *Applied Grammatology* a practice of creativity, frequently reminding us that the "post(e)-pedagogy" he advocates shifts emphasis from the transmission of information to invention. John Harned, though he articulates connections between deconstruction and process pedagogy that bode radical changes, finally steps back and takes deconstruction as a tool for invention that is quite clearly subordinated to a version of "our mission" of "stimulating our students to write better" (15).

Deconstruction in these pieces appears to have little bearing on what "essays" might look like, and leaves the familiar and unexamined aims of "improvement" toward "better" writing intact. It is precisely at this point, however, that deconstruction would and could intervene, for it is concerned with writing processes as they appear on the page and, importantly, writing processes that dismantle the forms of the book and the essay, processes such "unities" cannot "settle." Derrida attacks the kind of well-composed and unified essay we know, and refuses to grasp his own writing as " 'essays' whose itinerary it would be time, after the fact, to recognize; whose continuity and underlying laws could now be pointed out; indeed, whose overall concept or meaning could at last, with all the insistence required on such occasions, be squarely set forth" (*Dissemination* 3). He pursues textual operations and effects that exceed effects of unity, conceptual dominance, and control. Derrida's work is remarkable because of the features of his prose, with its digressions, recursiveness, equivocations, with its juxtaposed parts and multiple points and points of view, which irregularly and surprisingly mesh with, confront, and transform each other.

One of the reasons, surely, that such deconstructive writing has not touched what students finally present as their essays is the progressive process to which our thinking about writing is harnessed. The oppositions we typically use to make sense of (and contain) writing processes—for example, between "exploratory writing" and "formal presentation," or between "writer-based prose" and "reader-based prose"—are uncongenial to lessons of deconstruction inasmuch as they suggest that such "things" "exist" and that there are practices that will bring writing to an end by moving it from unsteady exploration and invention to conceptual mastery, airtight argument, well-made construction, and manipulative practices (presented as "aids" to readers). These oppositions look crude and misleading when they confront the complexities of writing, partly because (as everyone would finally acknowledge) exploration infects all writing, there are no clear divisions between "free writing" and premeditated control of an audience, and play among parts of a text and between texts goes on despite efforts to stop it.

They also look rigid and limiting when confronted from deconstruction, because their ends (fantastic or not) and tools work hard to foreshorten the possibilities of writing. Most of the advice given to students under the authority of the ideal of "reader-based prose" would be called immediately into question by a poststructuralist writing. The basic maxims for saving readers from difficulty, for easing their passage through a text, for avoiding excessive demands on short-term memory—that a writer "orient" readers by providing a telling title and using headings, guide them by quickly presenting an overarching thesis, use topic sentences to subordinate paragraphs to the thesis and to encapsulate units of meaning, provide periodic summaries that divide the argument into graspable stages—all aspire to a hierarchy and control that a poststructuralist perspective would consider delusory (because of the insecurity of pretensions to immobilize meaning) or unfortunate (because of the reductions such limits try to enforce, the dodges involved in their coherences, the manipulations and prescriptions enacted through their clarity).

This is not to say that a writing influenced by deconstruction would refuse such markers and devices, but rather that they would be treated always as parts of the general textual economy—not outside of it, not transcendent, not as external controls that would arrest "the concatenation of writing" (*Dissemination* 5). If presented as "outside" the text ("hors livre"), they come into circulation as additions of meaning, not reductions, not announcements of the author's mastery of the textual whole, and not distillations of the writing-to-come presented for the reader's possession. Within the general economy of the text—a shifting economy of moving parts that continually entail and encipher each other—a thesis would not be secure as an inscription of a restricted economy of meaning. Instead of serving as an arch or frame, it would itself be framed, turned into only a momentary effect: "Suddenly it is a part. And just as suddenly apart. Thrown back into play. And into question" (*Dissemination* 350). Indeed, any "*program*," Derrida would tell us—preface, thesis, map, topic sentence—is "already a pro*gram,* a moment of the text, reclaimed by the text from its own exteriority" (20). Similarly, Derrida would recommend (as he says Mallarmé does) a "*suspension* of the title . . . both because it raises its voice and drowns out the ensuing text, and because it is found high up on the page, the top of the page becoming the eminent center, the beginning, the command station, the chief, the archon" (177–80). But such suspension, stilling the overweening authority of the title, would not preclude its use as a generative source, a textual part radiating multiple possibilities of meaning, poised to combine with other parts of the text—"yet unreadable, protruding like a toothing-stone, waiting for something to mesh with" (289). Titles and theses become pieces in the play of meaning, not the rules of the game (330–31). A deconstructive pedagogy would promote a writing interested in, aware of, and ready to exploit such "gambols of language."

Hand-in-hand with the processes that are thought to bring writing to reader-based ideals are processes thought to bring writers to control of their texts—to self-assertion, and ownership, and masterfully autonomous shaping. The "empowerment of students" is an idea attractive enough (to us all) to make even crusading poststructuralists drop their notions that the writing "I" is always in process, always modifying and modified, continuously dislocated, knocked about by the repercussions of language. John Harned writes, with no apology, that in adapting and adopting deconstruction "we will resist the effort to dislodge the author as the authority who controls the shape of his or her text" (15). While Sharon Crowley's "writing and Writing" begins with an idea of a text as boundaryless, a flow of multiple, uncontrollable discourses into which a writer may enter, this is overborne by a democratic image of authoring as empowerment, and the essay slides past a vocabulary of self-determination into one of mastery that promotes students' faith in the intelligibility of their own writing. Other preservations of the writer's authority are commonplace in deconstruction's American guises. As Gayatri Chakravorty Spivak writes, deconstruction in the "narrow sense"—simply a "literary-critical methodology" that "fit only too well into the dreary scene of the mainstream pedagogy and criticism of literature in the United States"—locates the "(dis)figuring effect of a radical heterogeneity" in the "'text's' performance [not in the writer's self] and allows the critic authority to disclose the economy of figure and performance." Deconstruction "in the general sense," on the other hand, "puts into question the grounds of the critic's power" (16). Such throwing into question (as Derrida puts it) of the "consciousness of ideal mastery, this power of consciousness in the act of showing, indicating, perceiving, or predicating" (*Dissemination* 352) lacks practitioners. But perhaps the real point is that, just as we need a general theory that both respects the autonomous and purposive subject and acknowledges its divisions, constitution, and dissemination, so we need to face writing—including student writing—unbridled by the impulse to take sides on simple oppositions between empowerment and disenfranchisement, authority and uncertainty. This would entail, now, being much more ready to take language (I am again quoting *Dissemination*) as "a force whose effects are hard to master, a dynamics that constantly surprises the one who tries to manipulate it as master and as subject" (97).

How might such deconstructive writing practices and perspectives enter our pedagogy? I find uninspiring a hope for "assignments" or "exercises" that will add deconstruction to the classroom. This is not only because the existing suggestions are thin and practiced apart from everyday writing—see, for example, Sharon Crowley's suggestion to have students "write opaque prose once in awhile," play with sentence-combining, and experiment with traditional rhetorical devices ("Gorgias" 284), or Gregory L. Ulmer's student exercises in plagiarism and misreading ("Textshop" 58–59). It is also that, while the authority of the teacher cannot be denied, it perhaps can be loosened, but exercising the foresight of assignments and sequences does not move in that direction. A readiness to engage—in conference, in class discussion, in written comments—what comes to us in student writing promises something else. This may simply involve acknowledgment of and receptivity to difficulties our students experience, difficulties we may otherwise try to suppress or dismiss—that straddling a stretch of writing with a thesis does indeed pose problems, that the benefits for readability a thesis offers may run up against the impossibility of saying beforehand what a text in all its turnings undertakes, that texts often (always?) exceed anticipations and recapitulations, that writings often harbor many theses, that doctoring writing to suit a thesis requires repressions aplenty, that introductions and conclusions indeed *are* "hard" to compose—because of their suspicious pretensions to reduce a chain of writing to an idea, because they can provide only feignings of totalizations or final revelations. We may also add to our repertoire of questions to ask of writing: If we find a title that does not give us a "good idea" of what an essay is "about," what *does* it do? What does it do in relation to other parts of the text—this part, that part? If a text does not carefully restrict meanings by titles, theses, topic sentences, conclusions, and so forth, what happens in the writing, and in what ways might we evaluate what happens? Might there be benefits to a text that displays a writer's process of discovery and invention? In the case of texts that appear carefully composed or strongly gain our consent, where does a careful reading show conflict or lapses in univocity, and can a critical reading always point out in such student texts a "relationship, unperceived by the writer, between what he commands and what he does not command of the patterns of the language that he uses"? (Derrida, *Grammatology* 158).

I do not write the preceding paragraph to invite everyone to teach students to write like Derrida. The features of his styles that Barbara Johnson lists—unspeakable syntax, allusions, cryptic beginnings and endings, unconventional units of coherence (letters, anagrammatical and homonymic plays, puns), and so on (*Dissemination* xvii)—strike me as idiosyncratic moments that are less compelling as classroom matter than are the general implications of deconstruction and dissemination. And the most general implication is the marriage of deconstruction to a different "process pedagogy"—distinct from those with models of writing process that aim always for standard, sturdy prose. For deconstruction is akin only to versions of meaning-making process that see endless readings, reinterpretations, and recontextualizations overrunning every sheet of paper we, or our students, inscribe. Moreover, this understanding would be apparent in the writing. To extend deconstruction into student writing would mean taking student texts as never finished—in the sense of a smooth surface, a clinched argument, or a rounded discussion—but instead encouraging the rough edge that signals troubles, vexing complications, contradictions, allowing the insecure articulations that hover around an undecidability. The pretense of certainty a thesis has, the security of a conclusion, the assertion of mastery over a text would give way.

Seeing and teaching writing in this way, one might think, could be welcomed as a new purchase on the workings of language that is well suited to our historical moment. But of course it is not welcomed. W. Ross Winterowd, who more than any other writer on composition and deconstruction appears to grasp the implications I have been trying to foreground, attacks meshings of deconstruction and the teaching of writing precisely because they threaten the essayistic practices of our currently dominant tradition. In the composition classroom altered by deconstruction, he writes, an "endless dialogue and dialectic will replace conclusiveness: the clearly stated enthymeme, the clincher sentence of the paragraph, the crisp summary conclusion. For better or for worse, a change not only in attitudes and epistemologies, but also in practices" (86–87). This statement is almost neutral enough to invite endorsement, to rally encouragement for the developments it describes. As Winterowd elaborates his vision of a deconstructionist future, however, the unhappy edge takes over the essay. "Explanatory" writing and, Winterowd seems to think, any writing with claims of certainty or reference, "will be devalued in favor of others that fit the value systems of the poststructuralists" (90), until opacity and obfuscation will be most valued in student writing. In this poststructuralist nightmare, a refusal to communicate rules the day, and "gobbledygook and obscurity are enfranchised" (87).

Unintelligibility does not characterize writing carefully attentive and wise to its scatterings of meaning, nor does it characterize writing that displays a careful estimate of the tenuousness of its positions and of the writer's limited control over text, language, and signification. But to step back from Winterowd's particular lament and survey the broader territory: What can account for the general unwillingness to extend deconstruction past invention into forms of writing, the reluctance to treat student texts as objects of deconstruction, the failure to encourage self-awareness in student products of gaps, contradictions, exclusions, undecidabilities, multiple points of view? Some easily apparent forces, of course, work to preclude our teaching a Derridean Writing that refuses to totalize itself, that preserves multiple strands of coherence and play among them. There is the professor's institutional obligation to teach "serviceable" prose, joined to a strongly felt responsibility to our students to equip them for success. But it unhappily seems that with the renewed concern over general literacy has come, quite often, a resignation to a limited teaching, a diminished literacy of efficiency and know-how that employs language skillfully only on the job. As Sharon Crowley has written, "to confine instruction in composition to the writing of 'readable' prose is to prepare our students for careers as bureaucrats rather than as rhetoricians of whatever field or profession they might choose to enter" ("Post-Structuralism" 190). While we appear to handicap our students by not more fully fleshing out their knowledge about writing that is effective, communicative, clear, redundant, hierarchized, purposeful, and so on, we arguably do them another disservice by failing to point out the pitfalls of such writing (for example, the difficulty they already sense—that ingenuousness at best, and falsehood at worst, are the real securities of theses, arguments, and conclusions).

We may also cheat students by failing to teach other kinds of writing. If, to use Richard Rorty's phrase, philosophy is a kind of writing, and if, to extend the idea, English studies represent a kind (or, rather, overlapping kinds) of writing, then teaching students that there is only one kind of writing worth learning, an efficiently instrumental writing fashioned for the professional transmission of information, a writing increasingly unlike our own writing, is an acquiescence and a condescension. To be sure, critical practice in our profession has not moved decisively to a writing that mimics Derrida, and many may think it naïve—and not merely premature—to seek a freshman writing pedagogy akin to discursive practices embraced only by poststructuralist factions in the academy. However, if we are not emulating Derrida in professional journals, writing in our profession nonetheless includes, or is moving toward (or returning to), a writing of uncertainty, recursiveness, complexity, a writing that is especially and obviously *written*. Do we not have a responsibility to teach students this thinking-writing? If embedded in our best writing is an education about writing itself—its figurative, rhetorical, shifting capacities, its provisional place in the interweavings of other writings—then we are right to share this education with our students. We have, then, a range of reasons for teaching a writing that would forswear simple ideals of focus and thesis, undermine its own foundations, juxtapose incompatible discourses, play, and explore: namely, to promote a general awareness of the multiplicity of functions language performs; to allow for the possibility of other constructs and uses of language aside from those that preserve the fantasy of mastery and possession of packaged knowledge; to critique and learn to resist prescriptions in language for its interpretation and use; and more generally, to avoid a trivializing betrayal of what we have learned about knowledge and language, about the workings of interpretation and signification—about the uncertainties there, the tricks, ruses, and evasions.

To observe that an institutional obligation to teach serviceable prose stops us from teaching the writings suggested by deconstruction raises a political implication. Forms and styles of writing undoubtedly impose and uphold ideologies and social practices and relations. We may see here what Derrida describes when he declares that tampering with language and its presumed capacity to convey information forthrightly is more dangerous to the institution than "revolutionary ideological sorts of 'content,' " which do not "touch the borders of language" or the "juridico-political contracts it guarantees" ("Living On" 93–95). Cary Nelson, writing about theory in the classroom, notes that "much recent theory is concerned with the political effect of its writing practices," and the commitment of theory "is not to the technology of interpretation but to various forms of writing, not to schematic and easily teachable methodologies but to complex discursive practices" (xiii). If we can agree with this (and surely there are difficulties, connected with doubts about the political project of poststructuralism and the ideologies and practices *it* might sustain), then the move by which the implications of deconstruction for writing are bypassed, and deconstruction is instead classed next to invention heuristics and other technologies of reading, looks unfortunate but telling. We may come to think that, compared to the threat posed by altered discursive practices to a smoothly maintained social and ideological order, deconstruction as a technology of reading is only a pastime.

The question of political effect is pertinent especially because so many of the writers I have already mentioned see political implications in what they recommend. Atkins and Johnson, the editors of *Writing and Reading Differently,* suggest that their volume is a "symbolic and political act" (viii) and assert that deconstruction has the capacity "to effect change—in institutions, in disciplines, in individuals" (11). Crowley ends her essay "writing and Writing" with a call to use the empowerment of students to begin "the larger, the cultural project" (99). Kaufer and Waller's project of teaching reading and writing as the continual reconstruction and rearrangement of knowledge has a radical political subtext: that knowledge, because it is cultural, ideological, and continually produced, changes and can be altered. Gregory L. Ulmer hopes that the possibilities opened by Derridean Writing for invention will stimulate people to create not only on paper and in art but also "in the lived, sociopolitical world" (*Applied* 264). These writers appear to connect themselves to a politics often associated with deconstruction, a local politics of cultural resistance, subversion, demystification, the undermining of hierarchy—and perhaps of redefinition, recontextualization, bricolage—enacted in a struggle over image and language as part of an emancipatory project. But the apparent compatibility of their projects with the orthodox, or newly orthodox, in the teaching of writing raises the question: Are these writers, as the editors of *Writing and Reading Differently* admit they might be, "dulling and weakening what deconstructionists sometimes regard as a finely honed intellectual and even political weapon"? (10). Or (and here the editors quote Jonathan Culler) are they working "within the terms of the system but in order to breach it"? (2).

The general answer from the current ranks of deconstructionist-compositionists is that their work is a breaching, not a dulling or weakening—or at least that the weakening must be risked because the only breaching comes from within. The writers agree, that is, with Derrida's assertion that there is no outside to the system—to the institution and its apparatuses, practices, ideologies, languages (see Lietch 17–18). Teachers must derive their political effectiveness from their privileged position in the institution, can only take positions in relation to the structures that govern us, and must make strategic alliances (see Ulmer, *Applied* 169). As Gary F. Waller writes (invoking Foucault), "in order to speak meaningfully to and within a dominant discourse, we must be inserted within it instead of trying to create an alternative outside. Deliberately choosing to be marginalized is a kind of masochism, the root of martyrdom. . . . Discursive structures do change, but they do so from within a given state of affairs" (11). With such a predicament, of course, comes the risk of accommodation, institutionalization, acquiescence. This sense of our situation foregrounds our possible positionings in relation to established teaching practices—and points out that every pedagogical act involves a judgment about its relations to dominant forms of power and practice and either an assent or a resistance to this relation. If we grant these assumptions, one important matter is our analysis of the entry of deconstructionist practice into writing pedagogy, its relations to other pedagogical practices, and the implications of these relations.

When we see "deconstruction" as a term brought into our critical discourse, and yet see that under its name we receive the familiar, and can carry on writing as usual, what are we to think? Is this a case of strategic alliance, a tactful entry of important change into the powerful social apparatus of the classroom? Or is it complicity, assimilation, naturalization? The contrast between what looks like a radical philosophy and its translation into what looks like familiar writing pedagogies must at least make us consider the possibility that "deconstruction" in our writing about teaching has come mainly to represent only a minor deviation, one allowed within our institutional and disciplinary limits partly to resist larger changes. Perhaps, more starkly, deconstruction functions here as a myth of subversion in which effective difference is overborne by the differences of novelty. Perhaps adopting deconstruction as a technology of reading and as a practice allied with process pedagogy locates it where it can induce the least change and serves to render it easily assimilable into the existing classroom practices and order. If we still want to look to deconstruction to transform our writing pedagogy, we must take such doubts seriously and sharply question the ways it enters our thinking about teaching. If we want to engage the questions of deconstruction's practicality (questions this essay finally and necessarily leaves hanging), and if we want to test the political import and consequences of its discursive practices, it is time to bring deconstructive *writing* into classrooms and begin the examination of its effects.

Works Cited

Atkins, C. Douglas and Michael L. Johnson, eds. *Writing and Reading Differently: Deconstruction and the Teaching of Composition and Literature.* Lawrence: UP of Kansas, 1985.

Covino, William. "Making Differences in the Composition Class: A Philosophy of Invention." *Freshman English News* (Spring 1981): 1–13.

Crowley, Sharon. "Of Gorgias and Grammatology." *College Composition and Communication* 30 (1979): 279–84.

———. "On Post-Structuralism and Compositionists." *Pre/Text* 5 (1984): 185–95.

———. "writing and Writing." Atkins and Johnson 93–100.

Derrida, Jacques. *Dissemination*. Trans. Barbara Johnson. Chicago: U of Chicago P, 1981.

———. "Living On: Border Lines." *Deconstruction and Criticism*. Ed. Harold Bloom et al. New York: Seabury, 1979. 75–175.

———. *Of Grammatology*. Trans. Gayatri Chakravorty Spivak. Baltimore: Johns Hopkins UP, 1976.

———. *Positions*. Trans. Alan Bass. Chicago: U of Chicago P, 1981.

———. *Writing and Difference*. Trans. Alan Bass. Chicago: U of Chicago P, 1978.

Donoghue, Denis. "Relax, It's Only a Theory." *New York Times Book Review* 1 Mar. 1987: 14.

Harned, John. "Post-Structuralism and the Teaching of Composition." *Freshman English News* 15 (1986): 10–16.

Horner, Winifred Bryan, ed. *Composition and Literature: Bridging the Gap*. Chicago: U of Chicago P, 1983.

Kaufer, David, and Gary Waller. "To Write Is to Read Is to Write, Right?" Atkins and Johnson 66–92.

Leitch, Vincent B. "Deconstruction and Pedagogy." Atkins and Johnson 16–26.

Miller, J. Hillis. "Composition and Deconstruction: Deconstruction and the Teaching of Writing." Horner 38–56.

———. "The Function of Rhetorical Study at the Present Time." *The State of the Discipline, 1970's–1980's*. Ed. Jasper Neel. Special issue of *ADE Bulletin* 62 (Sept.–Nov. 1979): 10–18.

———. "The Two Rhetorics: George Eliot's Bestiary." Atkins and Johnson 101–14.

Nelson, Cary. Introduction. *Theory in the Classroom*. Urbana: U of Illinois P, 1986. ix–xvi.

Northam, Paul. "Heuristics and Beyond: Deconstruction/Inspiration and the Teaching of Writing Invention." Atkins and Johnson 115–28.

Rorty, Richard. "Philosophy as a Kind of Writing: An Essay on Derrida." *New Literary History* 10 (1978): 141–60.

Spivak, Gayatri Chakravorty. *In Other Worlds: Essays in Cultural Politics*. New York: Methuen, 1987.

Ulmer, Gregory L. *Applied Grammatology: Post(e)-Pedagogy from Jacques Derrida to Joseph Beuys*. Baltimore: Johns Hopkins UP, 1985.

———. "Textshop for Post(e)pedagogy." Atkins and Johnson 38–64.

Waller, Gary F. "Working within the Paradigm Shift: Poststructuralism and the College Curriculum." *ADE Bulletin* 81 (Fall 1985): 6–12.

White, Edward M. "Post-Structural Literary Criticism and the Response to Student Writing." *College Composition and Communication* 35 (1984): 186–95.

Winterowd, W. Ross. "Post-Structuralism and Composition." *Pre/Text* 4 (1983): 79–92.

11

The Exceptable Way of the Society: Stanley Fish's Theory of Reading and the Task of the Teacher of Editing

Elaine O. Lees

[A]lthough the person work can be understooded by society it must go under many other revision when the person gets older, so it will be under the exceptable way of the society.

By the person reworking his works from the first draft to become a mature creator, he must take some risks in finding out the excepted literature views that he must use in his society. This means that he must use punctuation marks by the way the society wants it to be used, not by the way he wants it. . . .

But if . . . he is in my position of not knowing how to express himself my using the exceptive method of the society, he would have pity for himself, he would be up late at nights asking God for his help. The person who is stuck in the literal stage, his written would be unorganized, and he would make simple mistakes. He cares about the mistakes, but it would hurt him so bad that he would just don't know what to do. While the writer that is not stuck would have some freedom in the way he wrote his works . . .

—Excerpt from a student's paper

No words spoken by writing teachers to their students more strongly imply the notions of community and exclusion, of acceptance and alienation, than the words *correct* and *error*.[1] These words resonate in peculiar ways with a concept of earned citizenship, with the belief that opportunity and respect may be won by those who strive for self-improvement, who master an unfamiliar language. Somewhere in this resonance, then, we hear the echoes of an American dream.

In this essay, I want to set such a dream beside Stanley Fish's notion of "interpretive communities," beside the behavior of ten members of a university's English department when they searched for errors in a student's text, and beside John Limon's discussion of Fish and Martin Luther King in the essay "The Integration of

Faulkner's *Go Down Moses.*" Through this conjunction of documents, I hope, first, to offer interpretations of the teachers' behavior; then, using Limon's work, to arrive at an amplification of Fish's stance on interpretive communities; and finally—by considering how students' growth as writers may be conditioned by students' power to imagine themselves *already* in community with their teachers—to suggest implications for the teaching of writing.

Let me begin with a look at where I think we are: with a glimpse of our commonsense wisdom on editing,[2] as that wisdom takes shape in a college handbook's chapter entitled "Editing Your Essay." I open with this passage because it provides a foil for Fish's position and embodies a familiar way to picture the task of error-hunting—a way I believe experienced writers ordinarily take for granted.

After the handbook's authors have listed techniques for tightening sentences, increasing coherence, and conforming to conventional formats, they offer their readers the following advice: "Before submitting your essay, you should check the manuscript to be sure everything looks and reads as it should. You must see exactly what is there—nothing more, nothing less. This is not so easy as it seems" (Heffernan and Lincoln 75).

Under ordinary circumstances most of us behave, I think, as if we share such a concept of editing. No matter what critical positions we occupy as scholars and teachers of literature, we speak as critical monists and naïve realists when we talk to students about error. We employ language that evokes an image of the task like the one the handbook evokes: proofreading is the activity of looking for "exactly what is there—nothing more, nothing less." A paper contains, right there in front of its readers, a finite number of errors. The errors are physically located in the text, among the "basic features" of the writing, the fundamentalist's province in the scriptural landscape. Skilled readers, really good editors, can therefore find those errors and say what they are, and rewrite the text so that the errors cease to exist. Our discourse thus treats error as a binary matter—either there or not there in texts—and it suggests that competent editors' reading is a binary matter, too: either competent editors will always find an error in a given spot in a paper, or competent editors will never find one there.

Yet the theories of Stanley Fish raise deep questions about this familiar image of editing. If we acknowledge, as I think we must, that reading for error is a form of reading for meaning, then from a perspective like Fish's we must deny that students' texts contain errors—at least in the way orchards contain apples and apples contain worms. Fish, like other reader-response critics, views readers as actively forming the meanings they see as in a text or on a page. For Fish, reading is not a matter of coming to see "exactly what is there—nothing more, nothing less." Rather, Fish sees readers as "writing texts, . . . constituting their properties and assigning their intentions." This act of "writing" requires that readers use "interpretive strategies," strategies for meaning-making that "exist prior to the act of reading and therefore determine the shape of what is read" (*Text* 171). Readers gain access to these strategies through membership in the entities Fish calls "interpretive communities." Because interpretive strategies are shared by groups of readers, a reader's "writing" of a text is never simply idiosyncratic.

By now, Fish's views are familiar in discussions of literature, though not in discussions of proofreading. I have argued at length elsewhere ("Proofreading as Reading"), however, that proofreading, like other reading, is an act of interpretation and criticism carried out within a cultural group. The activity of searching out errors in a text meets the conditions Fish outlines for acts of interpretation. First, it is grounded in the reader's initial act of "writing"—of constituting the text's properties and assigning its intentions. That is, readers locate an error where they sense a writer has failed to fulfill not simply local, but also text-wide intentions they have imputed. Second, it depends, for its coherence, on the existence of institutional structures within which utterances are seen as already organized with reference to assumed purposes and goals—in this case, adherence to conventional standards of correctness. Third, it draws on the community's knowledge of a discourse stipulating "identifying marks" (*Text* 304) and ways to argue that such marks are or are not present. This discourse includes such formulae as parsing procedures, mnemonic spelling aids, and rules found in handbooks and stylebooks.

Proofreaders, then, like other readers, construct, rather than uncover, meanings as they read. The difference is that we ordinarily regard proofreaders' constructions as more literal than literary. From a perspective like Fish's, however, it becomes harder to maintain that correctness and error are "exactly what is there" in texts; it appears that readers from different (editorial) interpretive communities—if such bodies exist—will "write" different texts when they read the "same" student paper, constructing different errors in them.[3]

Fish also makes it clear that interpretive strategies are learned, and they are learned through a process worth examining carefully.

To illustrate this process, Fish outlines a hypothetical classroom situation in which a knowledgeable student teaches her professor an interpretive strategy that will enable him to read a specific text as she does—in short, she begins to socialize him into her interpretive community.

> In the event that [upon her first use of a specific interpretive strategy] he was unable to identify the structure of her concerns because it had never been his (or he its), it would have been her obligation to explain it to him. . . . [S]he would have to make a new start, although she would not have to start from scratch (indeed, starting from scratch is never a possibility); but she would have to back up to some point at which there was a shared agreement as to what was reasonable to say so that a new and wider basis for agreement could be fashioned. . . . It is when such a [teaching] strategy has been successful that the import of her words will become clear, not because she has reformulated or refined them but because they will now be read or heard within the same system of intelligibility from which they issue. (*Text* 315–16)

One teaches someone the interpretive strategies of a community new to him, that is, by "backing up" to interpretive procedures the teacher and learner share. Pedagogy thus becomes a double activity, involving both an act of individuation ("What are the relevant strategies that I am enacting but the learner is not?") and an act of reconnection ("Where can we begin? What community, what interpretive framework, can function as our initial common ground?").

Later, I shall come back to the importance of pedagogy's double nature, as well as to Fish's views on deriving practical pedagogy from critical theory. Right now, we should note that, in Fish's example, when socialization into a new interpretive community succeeds, a teacher and learner come to share a second, expanded common ground. The learner now perceives a new set of "identifying marks" in texts, ones that previously the teacher alone could read into them.

For a student learning to edit his or her writing, I would suggest, these "identifying marks" include what we usually regard as texts' "surface features," as those features are understood by members of a community we might call "the (proof) readers of Edited American English." Uncertainty about these features is part, I think, of what troubles the writer whose text I quoted in my epigraph. This student knows from experience that others find mistakes—lots of mistakes, "simple" mistakes—in his texts. Though he entertains a rather subtle sociological view of his situation—he believes "the society" understands what his prose says but still deems it deficient in what he calls "the excepted literature views"—and though he accepts with real maturity the necessity to take risks and hazard guesses even though making small mistakes pains him, still, because his willingness to risk himself does not help him choose productive risks to take, he regards himself as "stuck" in a position outside "the society." He "just do[es]n't know what to do."

The student's conclusion, we should note, grows out of his critical position, a position that appears compatible with Fish's. Both views locate the student beyond a target interpretive community, place him in an outland, beyond the reach of a specific set of interpretive strategies that create agreement among readers and allow texts to be criticized. On one point, then, the three positions I have discussed in this essay may be said to converge. The "binary" notion of error outlined in the handbook, the student's faith in "the exceptable way of the society," and Fish's notion of interpretive communities all point toward the conclusion that readers trained in assessing Edited American English will see the same errors in a text. But this expectation may be naïve. The degree of unity within one such set of readers is the matter I will take up next.

Some time ago, a colleague and I asked ten composition teachers, all from the University of Pittsburgh's composition program, to participate in a study of error. As the first stage of the project, teachers had to underline every error they found in two student papers and label the errors in any way they saw fit. Figure 1 shows part of one student's essay, with the readers' underlinings collected under each word.

The collected underlinings allowed me to do a rather Fishian thing: to look at how members of what seemed to be a community of experienced editors responded to something that identified two student writers as Outsiders to that community, and to do so as if I could avoid privileging any reader's interpretation of what the papers "said." To obtain such a view, I constructed a graph, a visual metaphor for readers' responses to the two papers. In the graph, I considered each paper not as a temporal sequence of statements with meaning (not, that is, as a bunch of words and sentences), but as a string of consecutive spaces to which readers could respond. Each word counted as one space, each mark of punctuation counted as one space, and each space between words counted as a space, too. In Figure 2,

To me, his upbringing was well intacted. He got the best

education that his family could offered. He has good friends to

motivate him on through his years of learning. This was good ___

because without anyone to communicate to, then the learning

processes is weakened. That is why he missed his graduating

class because when they splitted up, then his friends were gone,

but he has learned to live without his friends.

Figure 1

Ten teachers' locations of error in a student's text. Each underlining represents one teacher's marking.

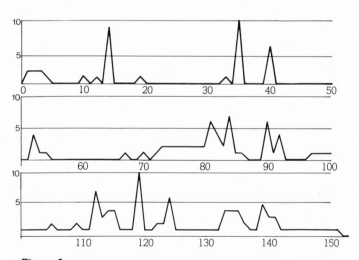

Figure 2

Graph of teachers' locations of error in the passage cited in Figure 1. Vertical dimension records the number of readers who found an error at a given space in the text.

for example, the word "To" (from the opening of the passage in Figure 1) counts as space one, the space that followed counts as space two, the word "me" counts as space three, and so forth. The complete paper from which this passage was taken adds up to 761 spaces. These spaces were indicated along the horizontal axis of the graph. I recorded on the vertical dimension the number of readers who indicated there was an error at each space.

By using this string-of-spaces concept, I could read the text as if its content were the yes/no reactions of ten readers over the course of 761 spaces. I could, for a while, then, step away from my own interpretation of the text as expository discourse by the student, and look at it as a convergence of ten readers' responses. I could thus get a kind of seismographic trace of the degree to which these readers saw error in given parts of the paper.

What we see when we look at the graph is, from any of the standpoints on editing I have discussed, rather surprising. We do not see the stately minuet (all dancers in, then all dancers out) that the "binary image" or the student's faith in the Society's way or the Fishian notion of a coherent community applying common interpretive strategies for Edited American English prepare us to encounter. Rather, we see something that looks more like a performance of *Lucia di Lammermoor,* with solos, duets, trios, sextets, periods of full chorus—and a divided family at the center. In fact, we see only 2 spaces where all ten readers note an error. (This passage is not unrepresentative. In the paper as a whole, only 16 of the 239 spaces marked by someone as erroneous were marked by eight or more readers.)[4] If error, then, is one thing that identifies the writing of those who are outside something we have come to call "the academic discourse community," it is also apparent from the ten readers' performance that these Insiders do not perceive Outsideness in the same degree and in exactly the same places in a given text. Rather, the signs of Outsideness are elusive; the frequency of underlinings suggests that most readers perceive a good many errors about, but in a given line they rarely agree on exactly where the errors appear.

The readers do concur in some instances, however. In 7 spaces in the paper, all ten readers find what they call an error, and in 522 spaces they agree that no error appears. When we consider those 7 spaces of perceived error along with the 522 spaces of agreed-upon correctness in terms of the whole paper, we see readers agreeing perfectly about two-thirds of the time. But the variety in what readers mark as errors is worth remarking. When we compare the 7 spaces of perfect agreement with the 232 other spaces marked as errors by at least one teacher, "what is there" appears considerably shaggier than the phrase "exactly what is there" suggests.[5]

To get a clue to how readers varied in their markings, I classified the marked spaces into high-, medium-, and low-vote spaces (3 marks or less = low; 8 marks or more = high), and then examined how readers' labels for the spaces differed. It turned out that the spaces marked as errors by eight or more readers appeared, by the labels raters gave them, to be what we might call "simple" or "rule-book" issues—matters one could look up in a dictionary or handbook and adjudicate with something like an algorithm. These spaces the readers labeled with words like "spelling," "subject-verb agreement," "tense shift," and "apostrophes." ("Missing words" also placed among the list of high-vote items.) On the other hand, the words readers used to label spaces few of them marked as errors—the little bumps on the chart—fell into a much broader range. They could, for instance, be the very words used to describe high-vote items-words like "tense shift" and "ungrammatical." But they could also be words that described judgments of style and order: words like "usage" or "logic"—or even "feels wrong."

Predicting high- and low-vote items on the basis of a single reader's underlinings or labelings was less than an exact science, then. But a pattern emerged when the ten readers' markings were compared: individual readers appeared to add to a shared "rule-book" a broad fringe of stylistic preferences and idiosyncratic rule applications, which they also used to locate "errors." And readers' level of teaching experience did not affect this pattern. Though the readers' experience teaching composition ranged from two to twenty-five semesters, every reader, from the newest teacher to the one who had taught writing for more than a decade, combined a small core of high-vote choices with a large fringe of low.

What kind of "interpretive community" can these ten readers be said to represent, then?

One can imagine a rather self-satisfied voice that would reply to this question by suggesting that the teachers in the sample are not quite competent detectors of error—that a better set of readers (say, ten full professors at Harvard) would produce more uniform readings of the texts. But such an objection misses the point. These ten readers are Insiders by definition: they have survived the trials to which the American university community, if community it be, subjects its novices. However diversely these readers read texts, their readings are not so outlandish, or outlandish in such ways, as to define them as Outsiders to the academic world.

And the fact that the readers are all Insiders has practical consequences for teachers and students. For instance, it calls in question the epigraph-writer's faith in the coherence of "the society"—in this case, a group of academics from his university—around a single "[ac]ceptable way." Their behavior suggests that considerable disunity exists among academic readers looking for errors in texts, even within one institution's writing program. What looks like an error to one teacher more often than not appears at least tolerable to another. It appears likely, too, that in conferences and classroom discussions the term *error* is used to refer to both high- and low-vote matters. Such variation must be puzzling to students moving from class to class—especially to those who believe they must master "society's acceptable way."

Much more than we assume, academic readers reading to locate errors may be—in Fish's terminology—"writing" different texts as they read. Why this should be so remains unclear. Perhaps some teachers locate error by focusing on what they think the text *says;* others, by focusing on what they think it is *trying to* say; still others, by focusing on what they believe it *ought to* say. But when one scrutinizes these categories, they shade into one another, leaving us with unanswered questions about what composition teachers construct when they create a reading of a student's paper. And behind this puzzle lies another, more fundamental issue: what it means to "belong" to an interpretive community, especially to a community whose discourse we have come to call "academic"—"the language of the university."

One way to approach the issue is to reconsider what it means to share a set of interpretive strategies. It may be that interpretive communities are not, as John Limon describes them, "bigger or smaller machines perfectly programmed (so [Fish] believes) for producing texts out of theoretical presuppositions" (422). Instead, readings of a single text by members of an interpretive community may bear only a "family resemblance" to one another: they may be related to one another through the repetition of significant features but may be far from identical—even when they perform the apparently "simple" task of locating error. Yet neither should they be viewed as departures from a single, ideal configuration. Recent statements by Fish seem to support such a position: in "Change," for instance, he argues that "it is the nature of an interpretive community" to be "at once homogeneous with respect to some general sense of purpose and purview, and heterogeneous with respect to the variety of practices it can accommodate" (432).

Confusion about Fish's stance on interpretation may grow out of a division in the way he discusses interpretive strategies. On the one hand, he argues that interpretive strategies "fix" readings. From this depiction, one might conclude (mistakenly, I think) that he regards interpretive strategies as something like computer programs played on human hardware, entities that crank out identical, socially determined readings of texts. On the other hand, as we have seen, Fish presents interpretive strategies as things taught and learned in human situations, through teachers' and learners' ability to move flexibly among interpretive systems until they locate a point of agreement, a patch of common ground, from which one party can begin to teach the other how to read the world in a new way.

John Limon points out an "apparent paradox" in Fish's position: "it takes unlimited supplies of understanding to build communities, but understanding itself is the product of communities" (425). Given this paradox, a question in practical pedagogy arises: if understanding creates community, but only community creates understanding, then how do Insiders and Outsiders *ever* locate the patch of common ground they need to develop a working pedagogy? In other words, how do Outsiders ever *begin* to become Insiders?

Fish suggests an approach to the issue when he argues that "the mind (and, by extension, the community) is an engine of change"— "not a static structure, but an assemblage of related beliefs any one of which can exert pressure on any other in a motion that can lead to a self-transformation" ("Change" 429). In other words, the interpretive machinery is itself dynamic. The mind/community endlessly works to turn phenomena (including unfamiliar interpretive strategies) into things it understands: "its assumptions are not a mechanism for shutting out the world but for organizing it. . . . [It] is always engaged in doing work, the work of transforming the landscape into material for its own project; but that project is then itself transformed by the very work it does" ("Change" 433). What starts out as a simple extension of an interpretive strategy may thus become an act of its revision. When that happens, the reader ends up not quite in a new community, but no longer limited by the interpretive boundaries of the old one.

Fish's second way of addressing the paradox of common ground involves breaking down the distinction between "outside" and "inside." An Outsider is not "*absolutely* outside," according to Fish, but "outside in relation to a set of assumptions": "his status as something or someone outside is conferred by the very community from which he is supposedly distinct; he is an *interpreted* outside" ("Change"

431). "Outsideness" itself is thus the product of interpretation; no such thing as a "real Outsider" exists.

This suggestion casts light on a passage by Martin Luther King, Jr., whose rhetorical strategy John Limon examines. The passage comes from the opening pages of *Stride Toward Freedom*. Here, according to Limon, King enacts an approach that enables him to work around the comprehension/community paradox that both he and Fish confront. From the beginning of *Stride Toward Freedom*, King refuses to accept the status of Outsider:

> The book does not open as one would have thought it should, with a grim illustration of the Montgomery scene before the bus boycott. Rather, it begins with King, already educated, already free, driving into the city: "On a cool Saturday afternoon in January 1954, I set out to drive from Atlanta, Georgia to Montgomery, Alabama. It was a clear wintry day. The Metropolitan Opera was on the radio with a performance of one of my favorite operas—Donizetti's *Lucia di Lammermoor*."
>
> And then the horrors of Montgomery hit him? No (two paragraphs later): "As we drove up to the church I noticed diagonally across the square a stately white building of impressive proportions and arresting beauty, the State Capitol. The present building was erected in 1851, and its high-domed central portion is one of the finest examples of classical Georgian architecture in America[.]" . . . The point is that King, as representative of Southern blacks, was already a member of the (implicitly continuous) European-American-Southern community. . . . (425)

Why does King choose this rhetorical strategy? According to Limon,

> King as author takes the risk of presenting a first glimpse of a black man in the South that is unexciting and even attractive, because the greater risk was admitting that the community he wanted did not yet exist. If it was not already in existence, it could never exist, since the understanding on which it could be founded needed its founding to be produced. (425)

One might consider the risk King takes, then, as a risk of appropriation: King enters the discourse of the empowered community—

masters its language—and from there turns to his own purpose its cultural landmarks, its pastimes and aesthetic concerns, its style of small talk. By demonstrating control of the discourse of the "(implicitly continuous) European-American-Southern community," this explanation suggests, King gains the right to a hearing—the right to begin to persuade the community to alter its boundaries.

Such a reading makes King's choice comprehensible, but it achieves that comprehensibility, we should note, by presenting King's risk as it might be perceived from *within* the European-American-Southern community, a community from whose standpoint King is the "interpreted other." An alternative reading of King's strategy suggests that the "risk" King takes is not appropriating power, but relinquishing it, by reducing the force of his "otherness," reducing his ability to stand rhetorically for a contradiction to the attractions of European-American-Southern culture. By entering his text humming *Lucia di Lammermoor* and admiring landmarks of Georgian architecture, King plays down his power as participant in an alternative discourse; he commits his text to establishing relations before clarifying differences.

To accomplish this purpose, King assumes his initial common ground with European-American-Southern readers—ground he can reclaim, "back up to," if necessary, as he teaches such readers a new way to see. And he does not simply "locate" that patch of common ground; he acts as though common ground (the Scottish manor in the Italian opera; the Georgian Capitol in the American South) is ubiquitous and habitable, despite its legacy as locus of struggle. Though Limon questions the coherence of King's position, one can hardly deny its rhetorical and political power.

King's linking of community and understanding, then, works both as rhetoric and pedagogy. First, King's assumption of community places him, in the opening of *Stride Toward Freedom,* within the European-American-Southern community. That rhetorical move— the move Limon refers to as "King's solution" (425)—appears to establish the "King" of the narrative in a powerful position—one we might call the "interpreted inside" (since in a Fishian view, no absolute inside is possible). It locates him and, not unimportantly, his readers within a community whose boundaries the narrative is designed to call in question. But it also represents a surrendering of power, a suspension of difference.

Second, by diminishing his otherness and fashioning a rhetorical connection to a way of seeing he would alter, the "King" of the passage acts as a Fishian teacher to his readers. King's pedagogy is founded on a denial—equally important for his black and white "students" to learn—of the substantiality of the boundary between the Outside and Inside.

At this point, King's solution intersects with the struggle of the writer of the epigraph. One barrier to this student's development as a writer, I would suggest, is his conception of "the society's" coherence about error. He is not quite, as he now regards himself, an Outsider to a coherent Society's ways, out of touch with something he calls (using the definite article) "the exceptive method of the society," "the exceptable way of the society." His situation is not so simple. To a degree the student cannot yet imagine, his "society's" ways are approximate, negotiable, revisable. This permeability is crucial to those who regard themselves as outsiders: to realize its implications is to know—profoundly—what motivation feels like, and how it converges with power.

For this reason, because it will free him to teach himself for himself, the writer of the epigraph must find a way to imagine himself as already in community with his teachers—to deny the substantiality of the boundary between the Outside and the Inside. By this, it should be clear, I do not mean that he needs to regard the teacher as his buddy, but that he must regard himself as *already* entitled to participate in the dialogue of the university—well before he has mastered the community's rule book. Taking such a step, when it is envisioned as a move from the Outside to the Inside, is not easy; it is agonizing. Though the act may look to a teacher like appropriation of power, to the student, it may mean surrender of the power of his difference, a betrayal of identities he regards as more real than the identity he will acquire.

By reinterpreting the issue of error, a teacher can prompt a student like the writer of the epigraph to begin reinterpreting his position in the academy. Basic information on the nature of reading, for example, can reassure students that they are not simpleminded or forever "stuck in the literal stage" if, at present, they cannot see what others see in their texts. A teacher can also acquaint students with a politics of error, by letting them know that not every academic reader who reads their work will see the same errors in it; because errors are not "exactly what is there" in a text, some errors will be more visible to more readers than others will

Both the diversity in readers' location of errors and their convergence toward a common "rule book" are conditions that writers benefit from recognizing. Students can be told that within the academy, as elsewhere, some errors are more "erroneous" than others: some editorial changes, like repairing spelling and verb agreement, are virtually mandatory; others, like preserving a smooth sequence in verb tenses and transitions, are common practice; and still others, like not beginning sentences with "and" or "but," are matters of stylistic preference. Writers can also be informed that in spite of general patterns in readers' responses, a given reader's response to a text may belie these classifications. The purpose of providing explicit, realistic instruction in the politics of error is less to raise students' editorial consciousness than to empower them to make informed decisions about where to focus their efforts.[6]

Denying that their differences prohibit participation in the university's discourse is far from the end of students' growth as editors, however. Editors, as they develop, learn new ways to read errors into texts. At this juncture, then, we need to consider how students learn editing itself, and whether Fish's theories help teachers devise instructional strategies to assist in that learning. Moreover, Fish's recent work raises two related questions: "Can instructional activities be said to be grounded in theories of interpretation?" And "Do anti-foundationalist pedagogies help learners develop as writers?" I will take up the recent issues first.

In "Anti-Foundationalism, Theory Hope, and the Teaching of Composition," Fish argues that no theory can be used as ground on which to build a teaching methodology. He contrasts his own position on this question with a "foundationalist" view, defining the latter as "any attempt to ground inquiry and communication in something more firm and stable than mere belief or unexamined practice. The foundationalist strategy is first to identify that ground and then so to order our activities that they become anchored to it and are thereby rendered objective and principled" ("Anti-Foundationalism" 65–66).

In contrast, Fish's theories (according to Fish) are "anti-foundationalist":

> Anti-foundationalism teaches that questions of fact, truth, correctness, validity, and clarity can neither be posed nor answered in reference to some extracontextual, ahistorical, nonsituational reality, or rule, or law or value; rather, anti-foundationalism asserts, all of these matters are intelligible and debatable only within the precincts of the contexts or situations or paradigms or communities that give them their local and changeable shape. ("Anti-Foundationalism" 67–68)

Any attempt to derive a pedagogy from, or ground a pedagogy in, theory is thus a foundationalist project—even if the theory in question is, like Fish's, anti-foundationalist. In an important sense, then, a pedagogy that claims derivation from his theory is self-contradictory; according to the theory itself, no such grounding is possible. Though Fish acknowledges that "as a card-carrying anti-foundationalist, [he] would certainly like to believe that the arguments to which [he is] committed will have a beneficial effect on the teaching of writing," he declares he must reluctantly remain skeptical—and do so because that response is "dictated by anti-foundationalism itself" ("Anti-Foundationalism" 70, 71).

One might question whether anti-foundationalism, as Fish defines it, can properly be said to "dictate" any practical application, including the maintenance of a skeptical attitude. But Fish's caution is nonetheless instructive. The "anti-foundationalist" composition pedagogies he discusses—ones that counsel "the teaching of anti-foundationalism, to ourselves and to our students" ("Anti-Foundationalism" 71) or that recommend "the analysis of the conventions of particular discourse communities" as the substance of writing instruction (Bizzel, qtd. in "Anti-Foundationalism" 74)—have gained currency in the profession over the past decade partly because they appear to address the fundamental problem of those students who are least at home in university classrooms—those students who seem most obviously "Outsiders" in academic circles. The approaches in question, which introduce students to discourse communities *as* discourse communities and show that community membership is achieved through the mastery of convention, share an underlying assumption: that examining a discourse community's conventions will enhance a student's ability to navigate within it. But Fish rejects this assumption on two counts: (1) we cannot perform the exhaustive analysis that would enable us to present the complete set of a community's conventions to students, and (2) if we accept an anti-foundationalist view, we cannot claim (or deny) on the basis of theory that a specific pedagogy, even a pedagogy that takes as its subject the "situatedness" of writing, will help learners to develop as writers.

Because his principal concern is whether theories imply pedagogical practices, Fish does not develop the possibility that accounts of discourse conventions—even when those accounts are the disputable, somewhat out-of-date descriptions that are the best any analysis can produce—may be of practical use to students. And yet, because in Fish's view theories neither imply nor rule out pedagogical methods, that possibility exists. Like the other sets of compositional rules,

maxims, and descriptions that, Fish argues, no theory may legitimate or exclude, an imperfect analysis of a community's conventions
may (though one cannot say it must) provide students with a guide,
"the precipitation of a practice" ("Anti-Foundationalism" 77), to con-
sult as they develop a practice of their own. A teacher thus may not
need to be in possession of an exhaustive description of an academic
community's assumptions in order to describe those assumptions
in a way that helps students more appropriately manipulate their
discourse within it.

But because no inevitable connection exists between discussing a
community's conventions and operating more skillfully within that
community, a more troubling possibility also arises: that analyzing
the workings of discourse communities may, under certain circumstances, impede students' developing practice. Here, it seems to me,
Fish's critique is most telling. Pedagogies that clarify how communities distinguish outsiders from insiders simultaneously rationalize
exclusions. Though some students may find this information a challenge to their powers of penetration, I suspect that others, less able
to deny the substantiality of the boundary between outside and
inside, will react with diffidence, not discourse. It is not self-evident
that examining the politics of discourse communities will encourage
a student—especially one who feels the lack of an acceptable public
voice—to write.

For individual writers, composition pedagogies are "productive"
or "counterproductive" in the words' most obvious senses, by encouraging or choking off the inclination to compose. In this context, Fish's
critique of "theory hope" underlines the appropriateness of what we
might call, for lack of a better theoretical term, pedagogical humility.
Amidst the tangle of situations that constitute a classroom, some
teaching methods will sometimes work with some students, and
others will not. No theory, in Fish's view, can reduce this condition
to a formula. Instead, "an anti-foundationalist hero," according to
Fish, ". . . can only enact his heroism by refusing to take either
comfort or method from his creed" ("Anti-Foundationalism" 77). But
even this act, it appears, reinvents foundationalism: the hero might,
with equal justification, refuse not to.

In the spirit of such a refusal, then, let me add a final observation
on the teaching of editing: by themselves, teachers cannot locate the
patch of common ground, the point of shared agreement, where a
student's growth as an editor can begin. The student must participate
in this process. In the heat of pedagogical speculation, of diagnosing
students' needs on the basis of our readings of their texts, we can

easily overlook this fact—perhaps on the assumption that writers who cannot yet perceive their errors surely cannot plan how to address them. As a result, we rarely have a sense of what conventions our students are curious about, or how they view their own uncertainties. Yet such points, where a writer senses a possible breakdown in "shared agreement" with his or her teacher about what is "reasonable to say," may be the place to begin a dialogue about convention. Having jointly defined a point of departure, and using whatever pedagogical tools and strategies are at hand, the teacher and learner can then proceed. As one student explained when she was asked how, in a matter of months, she had achieved growth as an editor that impressed her teachers and employer:

EB: What I've done was, um, had one of the secretaries here go through a book with me, a Gregg grammar book. I knew the parts of speech from learning it in school, but it's been a long time ago. And she, whenever we had a chance on our lunch hour, we would meet—sometimes once a week or once every two weeks—and she would go over, she would go through that, chapter by chapter—we never did get a chance to finish it, though, because we never had the time because she was busy, or I was busy.

EL: But you would meet on the lunch hour, and talk about it chapter by chapter?

EB: Chapter by chapter. And any questions that I would have— I have a way of making things more difficult than simple. In order for me to really get the understanding of what someone is trying to tell me, I have to tell them the way I see it, and they have to, let me see. . . . It's not like them saying, "Well this is the way it goes—this." I have to say, "Well you're saying that this should be here because—" You know? I have to do it that way.

EL: So you explained it back to her?

EB: Right. . . . I would tell her how I thought it was, and then if I was wrong, she'd say, "No, it would be this way." And she would explain to me.

EL: So she would teach by listening to you explain it? You would explain it back to her, and she would listen?

EB: Right. Right. She would listen.

(Berry, personal interview)

By consulting and building on the student's representations of her knowledge, the teacher—in this instance, the secretary who listened—formed a partnership that helped the developing editor define her uncertainties and teach herself. And though employing such a process made things "more difficult than simple," it also made it possible for the student, in her opinion, to "get the understanding."

The intriguing prospect for a developing writer may be, in the end, the possibility that someone will listen, that someone will hear what he or she has to say. A need to emerge, not simply to fit in, produces writing: a need to seem someone worth listening to, someone memorable—someone who appears, in the words of the epigraph writer, to "express himself," to "have some freedom in the way he wrote his works." Although the issue here, too, is community, it is community on a different scale.

As a result, the work that confronts the student editor is neither so difficult nor so simple a task as breaking and mastering "the society's" code. Though writers and their medium are constituted and sustained by community, those whose work is valued as their communities evolve are valued for reasons other than their adherence to convention. A teacher's task in teaching editing is to keep both sides of this constraint in view, and to assert—even before a student sees such affiliation as desirable—that the student already belongs to a group who gain (and give) something by wrestling with the written word.

Notes

1. The epigraph is from a paper by Christopher Cammock, to whom I am grateful for permission to quote. His essay was based on a passage from Howard Gardner's *Art, Mind, and Brain: A Cognitive Approach to Creativity*.

2. In this essay, the terms *edit* and *proofread* will be used interchangeably to refer to the processes by which writers locate and eliminate what they believe to be errors in their texts.

3. The question of how interpretive communities operate among editors is not much explored. One might read Diederich's classic study of variance among evaluators as related to this issue. Systematic, community-related differences also affect the location of orthographic and punctuational "error" by British and American read-

ers—though a healthy cultural relativism prevents these differences from being regarded as matters of correctness.

4. Out of a total of 1328 spaces in the second paper, 457 were marked by at least one reader as containing error. Of these, less than a quarter (103 spaces) were marked by eight or more readers.

5. I suspect that some of the variance in the readers' performances (though how much is unclear) should be discounted for the following reasons: (1) There may be a difference between editing competence and editing performance. That is, a reader in a given act of reading may not "see" all the errors that he or she "knows how" to see (via interpretive strategies). (2) Some classes of error, such as shifts in verb tense and problems in subject-verb agreement, affect several locations in a text and may be marked differently by different readers. Variations caused by such differences are methodological artifacts, and generate misleading patterns on the graph. (3) Readers may construct the same text with the same features, but disagree about whether a particular feature constitutes an error.

6. Before students can receive such instruction, however, teachers must know how to give it, and I am not sure that we do. Joseph Williams (1981) and Maxine Hairston (1981) have done preliminary work in this area. It would be useful to understand more about the things that "educated" or "academic" readers perceive as errors, so that we might (1) describe a politics of error to our students; (2) use a different nomenclature for low-vote and high-vote editorial matters in classes and conferences; and (3) refine our understanding of what it means to locate errors in a text. One problem in obtaining this information, of course, is the fluidity of interpretive communities. Even as a community's perceptions of error were being surveyed, those perceptions would be undergoing change. As a result, just as no survey could be used to establish an absolute standard of "correctness," no survey could be used to establish, once and for all, the statistical profile of a community's perception of error. What we would have, instead, would be an interpreted sampling of a moment in the community's development—but such a sampling might still be of use to teachers and students.

Works Cited

Berry, Eileen S. Personal interview. 29 June 1988.
Bizzel, Patricia. "Cognition, Convention, and Certainty: What We Need to Know about Writing." Pre/Text 3 (1982): 213–43.

Diederich, Paul B. *Measuring Growth in English*. Urbana: NCTE, 1974.

Fish, Stanley. "Anti-Foundationalism, Theory Hope, and the Teaching of Composition." *The Current in Criticism: Essays on the Present and Future of Literary Theory*. Ed. Clayton Koelb and Virgil Lokke. West Lafayette, IN: Purdue UP, 1987. 65–79.

———. "Change." *South Atlantic Quarterly* 86 (1987): 423–44.

———. *Is There a Text in This Class? The Authority of Interpretive Communities*. Cambridge: Harvard UP, 1980.

Gardner, Howard. *Art, Mind, and Brain: A Cognitive Approach to Creativity*. New York: Basic, 1982.

Hairston, Maxine. "Not All Errors Are Created Equal: Nonacademic Readers in the Professions Respond to Lapses in Usage." *College English* 43 (1981): 794–806.

Heffernan, James A., and John E. Lincoln. *Writing: A College Handbook*. 2nd ed. New York: Norton, 1986.

Lees, Elaine O. "Proofreading as Reading, Errors as Embarrassments." *A Sourcebook for Basic Writing Teachers*. Ed. Theresa Enos. New York: Random, 1987. 216–30.

Limon, John. "The Integration of Faulkner's *Go Down, Moses*." *Critical Inquiry* 12 (1986): 422–38.

Williams, Joseph M. "The Phenomenology of Error." *College Composition and Communication* 32 (1981): 152–68.

12

Afterword: A Rhetorical Ethics for Postmodern Pedagogy

Michael Clark

The essays in *Reclaiming Pedagogy* adopt a concept of human subjectivity that addresses one of the most intractable pedagogical problems of the last twenty years. Ever since the NCTE published its *Students' Right to Their Own Language*, teachers of composition have debated the political and ethical consequences of imposing on individual writers the various constraints of academic prose. Initially, the issue was cast as coercion versus integration, with liberal pluralists arguing the relative merits of various discourses and conservative pragmatists advocating a narrowly defined cultural literacy as the single avenue toward social mobility and economic success. Naïve as they were, these positions conceived pedagogical aims along the conventional lines of American politics, and this analogy politicized the teaching of English in a form recognizable to the public. Consequently, these alternatives continue to dominate public debate over educational policy today, even though the terms are conceptually obsolete and the positions useless as effective policy.

In the late 1970s, the attention of literary critics and specialists in composition shifted from the texts that students write and read to the processes by which those texts are produced. Out of this shift, there emerged a more subtle understanding of the relationship between linguistic conventions and the people who use them. By linking the various topics of eclectic programs in the continuous and often recursive process of the writer's own experience, the process approach promised a more coherent arrangement of the traditional concerns of composition pedagogy and guaranteed continuity among even the most public and the most private moments of the writer's task. Nevertheless, this approach did not seriously challenge the conventional separation of writing into discrete activities, and it retained the easy separation between autonomous writers and the coercive nature of linguistic constraints such as standardized spelling and grammar. Dividing "writing" into an array of activities linked sequentially along a temporal chain still allowed the influence of social forms to be relegated to a late and relatively trivial stage of the process. The writer's independence was preserved and exercised in pre- or "free" writing activities that served as the origin and inspiration of individual expression, while society remained exterior to that individuality as a force to be dealt with "later."

The product approach and the process approach differ radically in their pedagogical ambitions and practices. Nevertheless, as the editors of *Reclaiming Pedagogy* note, both models share a common notion of the writer as an autonomous individual whose subjection to the constraints of language is neither natural nor inevitable. Whether writing is treated as a product or a process, the writer's relation to the text is conceived as a voluntary capitulation to an external set of norms and expectations that constitute a form of social contract between the writer and the community. The terms of that contract may be as simple as standardized spelling or as complex as elaborate rules of evidence, but their common function is to constrain or repress the otherwise independent nature of human subjectivity.

Since students are free to accept or reject those constraints, both approaches force the teacher to arbitrate between the pragmatic goal of socialization and the humanistic ethic of personal freedom. The result, as the essay by Schwartz points out, is a paradoxical conflict between the way we teach students to think and the way we teach them to write. "Problems arise," says Schwartz, "when we direct our students to read complicatedly but to write clearly. . . . How can we invite students to see so much but to say so little?" Traditional approaches to teaching composition tolerate that contradiction because they render it invisible. As long as the writer is treated as independent of writing, the incompatible values attached to the two realms need not come into direct conflict. Yet the tension between them remains and is registered in the persistent concerns about bad faith and ideological consistency that plague the new teacher and bemuse cynical veterans.

Reclaiming Pedagogy makes that contradiction visible by rejecting the split between the writer and writing. Drawing principally upon the work of Michel Foucault, Roland Barthes, and Louis Althusser, the essays in this volume treat human subjectivity as a social construct, subject to the network of power relations that govern the circulation of discourse in society. Rather than treating the writer as an autonomous preserve of free will, these essays assume that the writer starts from a position within the social order and in fact is inconceivable outside of it. There is no question of capitulating to or escaping from that order because, as Foucault puts it, there is no "outside" to power. The dilemma posed by more traditional pedagogies is thus revealed to be a false problem, and the ideological choice between conformity or freedom is replaced by the strategic question of resistance.

For most of the authors represented here, resistance takes place in language. As the editors put it in the introduction, language is "the site of a power struggle," a field on which the student strives to wrest control from what Donahue calls the "cultural ghostwriter" of impersonal—indeed, antipersonal—discourse. Donahue goes on to describe the aim of this struggle as "empowerment," but it is not a struggle for freedom or control in the usual sense. Rather, it is a struggle among varieties of discourse, a realization of Bakhtin's "heteroglossia" as the fact and fate of human experience.

Instead of "liberation" or "self-expression," the pedagogical shibboleths of progressive composition theory for the past twenty years, *Reclaiming Pedagogy* invokes "irony" (Chamberlain) and "parody" (Klancher). These terms do not mark ideological positions but rhetorical attitudes that pitch one discourse against another and constitute the "subjectivity" of the author in—or even *as*—this discursive conflict. Thus Klancher concludes in his discussion of Bakhtin's work, "no one can write in a 'style of one's own,' and the aim of such teaching will be to reveal to students how much their own writing has been framed by particular stylistic practices they have absorbed unconsciously as monologic authority or—as one hopes—consciously as dialogic strategies."

The new mode of subjectivity motivating this goal requires as a corollary a new concept of discursive regulation, one that recognizes the productive aims of social constraint rather than its more obvious repressive functions. For as both Foucault and Althusser have pointed out, the primary ambition of ideology as such is not the repression of conflicting points of view; it is the production of a point of view that will facilitate its hegemonic control. Whether we call this production the "interpolation" of the subject, as Althusser does, or the "socialization" of the student, as more conventional, politicized pedagogies have termed it, the result is a subject or author created in the image of authority itself, not constrained by patterns of discourse but configured in their intersections.

Conceived in this way, power loses its status as restrictive rule and serves more as a generative principle for the production of discourse. This functional (and ideologically neutral) conception of power underlies most of the essays here and is especially apparent in the essays by Salvatori and Quandahl and in the editors' chapter "Freud and the Teaching of Interpretation." Though these essays differ considerably in their methodological orientations, they all treat reading and writing as essentially productive activities. Rather than having students simply model their writing on exemplary texts, the authors of these essays encourage students to treat those texts as a cross-section of the moment of their production. In place of an omniscient author and a coherent, immutable text, there lies a congeries of paths not taken, options denied and doubts unspoken. (As Knoper points out, this is the text of deconstruction, though it is read here as an arena of social conflict rather than the textual "differance" celebrated by literary theory a decade ago.)

The authority of the text thus appears against a background of silent yet viable alternatives, any one of which may be activated by the students as "counter-memory" that can produce its own discursive authority. The result is an endless proliferation of discourses, each born out of but not restricted to an intersection with the original—actually now the originating—text. Foster describes this pedagogical technique as "reading against authority," and he claims that it enables the student to "speak *with* authority" in the sense of speaking both "to" and "with" the authoritative role that situates the individual as subject in the symbolic order of discourse. These several senses of speaking with authority are summed up effectively in Schwartz's account of the new pedagogy as "conversation." Arguing that the metaphor of conversation should replace "reception" as the relationship between readers and writers, Schwartz notes that conversation requires that we give up "a particular kind of closure or certainty: . . . And the substitute I receive in exchange for the old certainty is a new role, one constituted by a responsibility to another."

This ideal of responsibility is not exactly analogous to the "resistance" advocated by the politicized pedagogies of the 1970s. Disseminative and pluralistic rather than collective and universal, tactical and strategic rather than ideological and altruistic, *Reclaiming Pedagogy* describes not so much a politics of composition as what might more accurately be called a rhetorical "ethics" after Jean-François Lyotard's use of that term in *Au juste*. There Lyotard proposes a new kind of collectivity for the postmodern world, one that "finds the raw material for its social bond not only in the meaning of the narratives it recounts, but also in the act of reciting them" (22). In our time, Lyotard argues, the social bond is essentially linguistic (*langagier*), and its history consists only in the serial recitations that perform the narrative through time. Thus, unlike traditional societies, which might be bound together by a shared sense of the past or even a devotion to a common discourse, the postmodern community "is not woven with a single thread. It is a fabric formed by the intersection of at least two (and in reality an indeterminate number) of language games" (40).

According to Lyotard, all of those games are different, but they share a common rule. In each case, the rhetorical address that constitutes the language games as such always involves "the obligation to reply," and it is this rhetorical obligation that constitutes the possibility of justice in a postmodern world. For it is not simply the necessity of a reply that Lyotard describes, but an obligation to "retell," to repeat the address and reproduce the social bond that it performs. I may not have to respond to the one who addresses me, Lyotard notes, "but I am obligated in the way of a relay that may not keep its charge but must pass it on" (35).

It is in this charge to "pass it on" that *Reclaiming Pedagogy* finds its inspiration and its mission. Conceiving the social bond as sheer fluency, the essays in this volume equate social responsibility and discursive response, political authority and the role of the author. Unfortunately, without a clear and explicit model of social organization that would justify a politics of conversation rather than confrontation, many of the essays in this volume tend toward what Edward Said has called the "worldless" quality of contemporary literary theory. The reductive and idealist overtones of the equation between politics and rhetoric at times vitiate the sense of urgent commitment that pervades these pages, and they threaten to trivialize the editors' self-confessed "visionary" ambitions. As Knoper points out in his essay, the alliance between composition and deconstruction may not be as radical as it sounds, and deconstruction may in fact be imported into composition theory "as a myth of subversion in which effective difference is overborne by the differences of novelty."

Yet, as its close affinity to Lyotard's work suggests, *Reclaiming Pedagogy* does not simply propose to apply new methods to old problems. By treating the subject's place in the symbolic order of discourse as essentially rhetorical rather than as a question of free will or ideological coercion, it shifts our sense of the "political" from the elusive threshold between individual and society to the concrete activity of reading and writing. That shift renders moot the charges of empty formalism or ideological complicity that have plagued the fields of both composition and literary theory since the 1960s. It also confounds the easy opposition of materialism and idealism that characterizes more conventionally politicized pedagogies today, and it sets the stage for a more local pedagogy that acknowledges the infinitely plural and irremediably specific character of all our lives. For in the end, all of these essays insist on our common bond with the writers we teach as well as the writers we read, and on the "obligation to reply" that Lyotard claims is the only possibility for justice left to us. Whether we call that bond political, ethical, rhetorical, or even pedagogical, it constitutes both the social order to which those students aspire and the visionary freedom of which their teachers dream. If we can meet our responsibility to pass along that obligation, we may yet write the history in which those alternatives are joined.

Works Cited

1. *Students' Right to Their Own Language, College Composition and Communication* 25 (Urbana: NCTE, 1974) 32 pp.

2. *Au juste* (Paris: Christian Bourgois, 1979), translated as *Just Gaming* by Wlad Godzich, with an introduction by Samuel Weber, Theory and History of Literature 20 (Minneapolis: U of Minnesota P, 1985).

Index

Index

173